Careers.

371 425

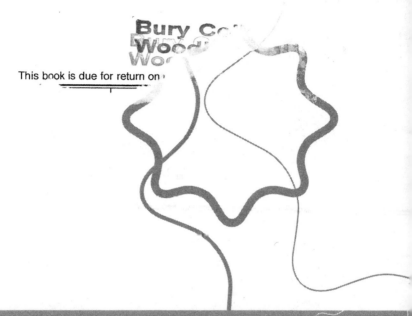

Succeed at psychometric testing

PRACTICE TESTS FOR

THE NATIONAL POLICE
SELECTION PROCESS

New edition

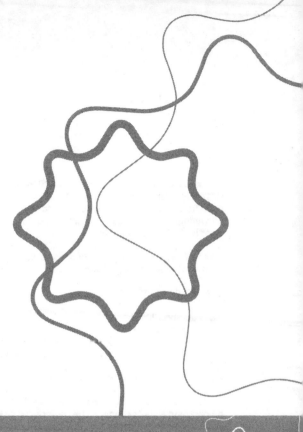

Succeed at psychometric testing

PRACTICE TESTS FOR

THE NATIONAL POLICE
SELECTION PROCESS

HODDER
EDUCATION
PART OF HACHETTE LIVRE UK

Bernice Walmsley

New edition

The publisher has used its best endeavours to ensure that the URLs for external websites referred to in this book are correct and active at the time of going to press. However, the publisher and the author have no responsibility for the websites and can make no guarantee that the site will remain live or that the content will remain relevant, decent or appropriate.

Orders: please contact Bookpoint Ltd, 130 Milton Park, Abingdon, Oxon OX14 4SB. Telephone: (44) 01235 827720. Fax: (44) 01235 400454. Lines are open from 9.00–5.00, Monday to Saturday, with a 24-hour message answering service. You can also order through our website www.hoddereducation.co.uk.

British Library Cataloguing in Publication Data
A catalogue record for this title is available from the British Library.

ISBN: 978 0 340 96926 7

First Published 2005
Second edition 2008
Impression number   10 9 8 7 6 5 4 3 2 1
Year   2012 2011 2010 2009 2008

Typeset by Servis Filmsetting Ltd, Longsight, Manchester.
Printed in Great Britain for Hodder Education, part of Hachette Livre UK, 338 Euston Road, London NW1 3BH by Cox & Wyman Ltd, Reading, Berkshire.

Hachette Livre UK's policy is to use papers that are natural, renewable and recyclable products and made from wood grown in sustainable forests. The logging and manufacturing processes are expected to conform to the environmental regulations of the country of origin.

CONTENTS

FOREWORD

Should anyone tell you that a psychometric test will give an accurate indication of your level of intelligence, don't pay too much attention. It isn't necessarily true.

The credibility of the global psychometric testing industry rests on the belief of employers that a psychometric test will yield accurate and reliable data about a candidate's ability. Busy employers buy into the notion that a psychometric test will swiftly eliminate all the unsuitable candidates and deliver up only the best, brightest and most able candidates to the interview stage.

What is not widely known is that it is perfectly possibly for a candidate to drastically improve their own psychometric score by adopting a methodical approach to test preparation. The purpose of the *Succeed at Psychometric Testing* series is to provide you with the necessary tools for this purpose.

It is useful to know that a candidate's ability to perform well in a psychometric test is determined by a wide range of factors, aside from the difficulty of the questions in the test. External factors include the test environment and the professionalism of the test administrator; internal factors relate to the candidate's confidence level on the day, the amount of previous test practice the candidate has and the candidate's self-belief that they will succeed. While you cannot always control the external factors, you can manage many of the internal factors.

A common complaint from test takers is the lack of practice material available to them. The titles in the *Succeed at Psychometric Testing* series address this gap and the series is designed with you, the test taker in mind. The content focuses on practice and explanations rather than on the theory and science. The authors are all experienced test takers and understand the benefits of thorough test preparation. They have prepared the content with the test taker's priorities in mind. Research has shown us that test takers don't have much notice of their test, so they need lots of practice, right now, in an environment that simulates the real test as closely as possible.

In all the research for this series, I have met only one person who likes – or rather, doesn't mind – taking psychometric tests. You are not alone. This person is a highly successful and senior manager in the NHS and she has taken psychometric tests for many of the promotions for which she has applied. Her attitude to the process is sanguine: 'I have to do it, I can't get out of it and I want the promotion so I might as well get on with it.' She always does well. A positive mental attitude is absolutely crucial in preparing yourself for your upcoming test and will undoubtedly help you on the day. If you spend time practising beforehand and become familiar with the format of the test, you are already in charge of some of the factors that deter other candidates on the day.

It's worth bearing in mind that the skills you develop in test preparation will be useful to you in your everyday life and in your new job. For many people, test preparation is not the most joyful way to spend free time, but know that by doing so, you are not wasting your time.

The *Succeed at Psychometric Testing* series covers the whole spectrum of skills and tests presented by the major test publishers and will help you prepare for your numerical, verbal, logical, abstract and diagrammatic reasoning tests. The series now also includes a title on personality testing. This new title will help you understand the role that personality testing plays in both the recruitment process and explains how such tests can also help you to identify areas of work to which you, personally, are most suited. The structure of each title is designed to help you to mark your practice tests quickly and find an expert's explanation to the questions you have found difficult.

If you don't attain your best score at your first attempt, don't give up. Book yourself in to retake the test in a couple of months, go away and practise the tests again. Psychometric scores are not absolute and with practice, you can improve your score.

Good luck! Let us know how you get on.

Heidi Smith, Series Editor
educationenquiries@hodder.co.uk

Other titles in the series:

Critical Verbal Reasoning
Data Interpretation
Diagrammatic and Abstract Reasoning
Numerical Reasoning Intermediate
Numerical Reasoning Advanced
Personality Testing
Verbal Reasoning Intermediate
Verbal Reasoning Advanced

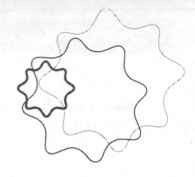

CHAPTER 1
INTRODUCTION

WHO SHOULD READ THIS BOOK?

This book is aimed at anyone who is considering applying for entry to a police force in England or Wales. To become a police officer you will have to successfully negotiate the new National Selection Process, which was introduced in 2004. Although we now have a selection process that Is the same throughout England and Wales, recruiting is carried out by each individual force. This means that there is now a common selection procedure and common entry requirements.

The test process starts with comprehensive application forms, then goes on to a variety of tests at an assessment centre. This includes tests to discover your abilities in the areas of written communication, numerical reasoning, logical reasoning, and other competencies that are needed in police work. But, make no mistake, it is possible to improve your score. Of course, the people who devise and publish these tests and the people who administer them don't publicise this fact. Publishers' sales depend on their clients believing that the results of the tests will guide them to the best candidates for the jobs on offer. The mystique of tests must be maintained.

There is no doubt that psychometric testing is not as straightforward as measuring your height or weight – your score may well change from day to day. Lots of factors will affect your performance including lack of confidence, stress, the conditions in the testing venue and so on, so your test score on the day can only ever be an indication or estimation of your ability. This fact is sometimes forgotten and tests given greater credibility than perhaps they deserve but they are certainly something that you can prepare for and by doing so improve your performance. With practice you can get rid of some of the stress and lack of confidence and other barriers to success. In the next section we'll look at five factors that can affect your score on the day.

Testing yourself on actual examples of the types of questions and tests that you will encounter is vital. Then, and only then, can you assess where your efforts to improve need to be concentrated.

In this book there will be a little theory about each of the types of tests and then plenty of practice. Not only will you improve the scores you can achieve in the National Test but the familiarity that comes from the extended practice available in this book will also raise your confidence level overall. This extra confidence will help to improve your general performance at interview. You will find lots of examples for you to work through and some handy tips on how to tackle them. We will be examining the common pitfalls associated with these tests and then discovering how to avoid them.

HOW CAN I IMPROVE MY SCORE?

It is perfectly possible to improve your score by your own efforts. The aims of this book are therefore two-fold – to improve your performance in the police assessment by providing you with the practice you need and also to help you to lessen the impact of the factors that will affect your chances of success.

Before we go on to the main body of this book – the practice and explanations of the tests – let's look at these factors that may affect your chances of success:

BELIEF IN YOUR ABILITY

This is about self-confidence. Research shows that a high expectation of success can be an important factor in getting a higher score. If you can get to the point where you know that you are well prepared and competent then you will improve your chances of success. This is because feeling confident increases the quantity of the type of hormones in your bloodstream that help you to focus. If, on the other hand, you're convinced that you will fail, then different hormones will make you anxious and less able to focus.

FAMILIARITY

Extensive evidence of the impact of coaching and practice on performance in a variety of examinations show that it improves results dramatically. Study carefully all the material you receive from the assessment centre. In addition to this, the large quantity of practice questions in this book will certainly give you the advantage of familiarity.

SPEED

Speed rather than accuracy is what is most important in most of the tests that you will take – although it's worth saying here that wild guesses are very rarely useful. Speed is important because of the way scores are evaluated and compared with others so only a slight improvement in your performance will dramatically improve your final evaluation. So, the more questions you answer the more chance you have of getting that vital extra point or two.

In view of the need for speed, the best advice is:

- Always answer as many questions as possible
- Go for speed not accuracy – but concentration is still essential
- Never spend too much time on any one question

UNDERSTANDING

It is vital that you understand completely what is required of you in the test. You will not get a good score if you do not follow instructions and understand precisely what you are meant to do. For this reason it is worth practising the various types of test and, of course, reading the instructions carefully.

ENVIRONMENT

This is an element of the tests over which you have little control. It may be quite busy at the assessment centre you attend. Practising at home may be good preparation for this eventuality as life will still go on around you while you are practising.

Having said that, the correct environment is certainly a factor in your getting the best score of which you are capable, so do not be afraid to complain if things are not right – it is likely that serious problems will be taken into account when assessing your performance if they are brought to the attention of the test administrator.

HOW AND WHEN WILL YOU SIT THE TESTS?

The National Selection Process for the police forces of England and Wales has a number of stages that you have to get through in order to be accepted into the police force of your choice. It is therefore vital that you give your very best performance throughout this process. The path to becoming a police officer is a long one with many tests and a lot of training along the way. Here is a rundown of the stages that you will have to get through:

1 A self-selection form – this can either be done in writing (by requesting details from the force that you wish to join) or you can do this online at www.policecouldyou.co.uk. This is a quick exercise addressing questions about eligibility criteria such as age, health, nationality and so on. On this website you can also check the current recruiting position for any force. If it is not currently recruiting you could experience a delay with your application.

2 The application form – this is an extensive document that must be completed extremely carefully.

It should go without saying that you should read the whole of the application form very carefully (including the guidance notes that are provided) before you start to complete it. It is an involved document that, properly completed, should ensure that you are called to an assessment centre.

3 The assessment centre – this is when you will take the written tests, activities and interviews that will assess your suitability for the role of police officer. All the exercises are designed to reflect your potential future performance. The assessment lasts for approximately 5 hours. NB: An assessment centre is not a place – it's a process.

4 Medical examination and security checks – this includes an eyesight check and taking up the references that you have had to provide on the application form.

5 Physical fitness test – this can be quite arduous and you should make sure that you improve your fitness if you feel it necessary before the assessment. This test consists of three parts – endurance, dynamic strength and grip strength. For more details about the fitness requirements and how you can prepare, consult the booklet you will receive with your application form.

6 Probationary period including foundation training – this is the intensive training that you will receive during your two-year probationary period before you can qualify as a police officer.

The most comprehensive test of your abilities will be carried out during the assessment centre, so let's look in a little more detail at what happens. Police forces – in common with most other large employers – use standardised tests as a technique to help them select the best candidates. If you meet the requirements of the application form, and there are appropriate vacancies in the force to which you have applied, you will be invited to take part in an assessment centre. The main purpose of this book is to help you with your preparation for the assessment centre.

The Entrance Assessment is a series of standardised, baseline tests and exercises that are timed and will include:

- Numerical reasoning test
  Verbal logical reasoning test
- Competency-based structured interview
- Written exercises
- Interactive exercises

During these tests and exercises you will be observed and your performance assessed against preset criteria. The aim is to assess your potential future performance. Your results from the selection assessment centre are sent to the police organisation that is dealing with your application and it will pass them on to you.

WHAT SORTS OF TEST WILL YOU BE GIVEN?

As we have seen, the National Selection Process is divided into five distinct parts. These tests and exercises are all designed to assess your abilities in the core competencies that the police authorities have deemed essential for success in the role of police officer. During the Selection Process the aim of the assessors is to decide whether or not you possess the potential to become a competent police officer.

As you will see from the booklet that you will receive with your application form, the role of a police officer in today's world is a far from easy one. The tasks involved in the role are wide-ranging and often difficult; therefore the abilities needed to cope with the tasks have had to be carefully defined to ensure that the right candidates are chosen. There would be little point in selecting a candidate who was unable to cope with situations such as staying calm in the face of racial abuse, or telling a child that his parents have been killed by a drunken driver. Not only would this result in an inferior police service but also the ill-equipped candidate would find the job intolerable.

There are many difficult issues that a police officer has to face, and unless new recruits are in possession of all the abilities, skills and character traits that the selection process demands – the core competencies – then they will not be successful.

These core competencies are:

1 Respect for race and diversity

2 Teamworking

3 Community and customer focus

4 Effective communication

5 Problem solving

6 Personal responsibility

7 Resilience

All the tests and exercises, in addition to parts of the application form, include assessments about your abilities in the area of these core competencies, and so it is vital that you understand fully what they mean and how they can be used to assess your stronger and weaker points. It is therefore worth looking in a little more detail at these core competencies and what they involve before we examine the tests and exercises.

1 RESPECT FOR RACE AND DIVERSITY

Throughout the tests and exercises you will have to demonstrate that you treat everyone with respect and dignity – no matter what their race, religion, background, status or position, ethnicity, appearance or circumstances. This is considered to be a very important aspect of every candidate's character, and all the exercises that you undertake will include assessment on whether or not you have displayed the appropriate respect for diversity. You should therefore think carefully about your answers in all circumstances, and make sure that your answers, remarks and actions do not contain anything that will let you down.

For example, during the interactive exercises be careful not to make any assumptions based on prejudice or narrow opinions. You must ensure that you present a view of yourself that shows that you respect differences and understand other people's points of view. You can put over this sort of impression by using language in an appropriate way, and by making people feel valued by listening to them and supporting their needs and interests. You should try to encourage people to 'open up' to you by being understanding and showing sensitivity to their problems, vulnerabilities and needs. Part of a police officer's duties will involve delivering difficult messages and bad news to all sorts of people so you should try to display your ability to do this by being both honest and sensitive. And, of course, you should respect confidentiality at all times.

During the assessment centre, the assessors will be on the lookout for any negative indicators that may be present in your behaviour, conversation or demeanour. In the area of respect for diversity, this would include behaving in an aggressive or overpowering way or perhaps showing humour in inappropriate circumstances. Do not allow indications of thoughtless, impatient or tactless behaviour to creep into your answers to questions or into how you conduct yourself during the exercises. Do not, under any circumstances, show bias or prejudice when dealing with people. Any of these negative signals will ring warning bells to an assessor and you will fail this very important aspect of the selection procedure.

2 TEAMWORKING

Here you have to show that you can work as a team member and that you will work together with others to achieve common goals. A good teamworker will have the ability to break down barriers between groups and will involve others in discussions and decisions. Try to demonstrate your ability to communicate and cooperate with the people that you are required to work with during the exercises. You must try to give the impression that you make time to get to know people and will be able to develop mutual trust and confidence. To do this you will need to be open and approachable and be ready to offer help whenever appropriate. It is also important to ask for and accept help when needed. If you were to act as if you could manage any task alone and were reluctant to ask for help, you would not be judged to be a team player.

Negative indicators that the assessors will be looking out for include not letting people say what they think, keeping information to yourself, taking credit for successes without giving credit for the contribution made by others in the team, and being reluctant to volunteer to help. Be aware of these ways in which you can let yourself down and make sure they do not appear in your answers or in your behaviour.

3 COMMUNITY AND CUSTOMER FOCUS

In order to do their job, police officers must understand the community they serve and have a commitment to policing a diverse society (there's that important aspect of police work again – diversity). Your focus at all times should be on the customer so that you will be able to provide the tailored service they need. This will involve sorting out customers' problems as quickly as possible while keeping the needs of the organisation you work for in mind.

An important way of dealing with a customer's problem, which will show your commitment to customer service, is to keep the customer informed at every stage as to what you are doing to resolve their problem and the progress you are making. If you can manage the customer's expectations and ensure that they are satisfied with the service they receive, you will have dealt with the problem successfully. If you make a mistake, then you must be prepared to apologise straight away and to sort out the situation without delay.

For all the situations into which you are put during the assessment centre, you must remember that you should treat the people that you have to deal with as customers and try to put their needs and safety before other, more minor considerations.

Remember too that in real life you would be part of a community and you would need to be able to get along with all types of people. This will inevitably include people of different races and cultures, and your approach to them must show that you are aware of the diversity but are able to act appropriately. You must understand what causes offence to different people and change your actions accordingly.

Again, there will be negative indicators that the assessors know to look out for. If you were to present an unprofessional image or to show little interest in the customer, then you would not get good marks in this core competency. A lack of understanding of the cultural or religious beliefs of different cultures will not be well received by the assessors, nor will a lack of sympathy or consideration to such differences in the community.

4 EFFECTIVE COMMUNICATION

This competency is obviously essential to a police officer in dealing with the public and with their colleagues. You must be able to communicate effectively both verbally and in writing. This involves listening carefully and using questioning techniques to make sure that others understand what is going on. You must be able to transfer effectively a huge variety of information and ideas to varied audiences – adapting your approach to suit the audience.

Clear communication is of paramount importance and, while giving an impression of confidence and authority, you must ensure that your message has been received correctly by your audience whether this is one lost child or a customer with a complaint or a rowdy bunch of teenagers. This means that you must change your style of communication to suit the situation, so that you meet the needs of the person or people that you are addressing. It will also involve explaining decisions where necessary and giving clear instructions in some circumstances. To ensure that you have got your message across in almost any situation you could summarise the information then ask one or two questions to check understanding. If you are giving any sort of presentation – maybe verbally to a formal audience or in writing in the form of a lengthy report – it can be useful to use the 'three tell 'ems'. This, of course, means that you take three attempts to put your points:

1 Tell 'em what you're going to tell 'em

2 Tell 'em

3 Tell 'em what you've told 'em

This translates into a solid structure for any presentation so that you can ensure you have a beginning, a middle and an end.

Try not to let your nervousness during the assessment centre make you rush or mumble your words. Speak slowly and clearly and, in written exercises, write as neatly and legibly as time allows.

The negative indicators that the assessors will be looking for can be split into two groups – those relating to verbal communication and those relating to written communication:

1 When communicating face to face try not to display any hesitancy, nervousness or uncertainty. A lack of confidence in your voice will soon translate into a suspicion in the people with whom you are dealing that you do not know what you are doing. A police officer is often in a position of trust and many people will be looking to an officer for help, so confidence and firmness are important. If you avoid answering difficult questions or are reluctant to answer questions fully without lengthy questioning, this will also ring alarm bells in the minds of the assessors.

2 In written communication a poor result would be obtained if you submitted an unstructured piece of work displaying poor spelling, grammar and punctuation.

5 PROBLEM SOLVING

Police officers are required to gather lots of information from many different sources and they must then analyse this information to identify problems and issues. You will then need to show that you can use this information to make decisions about how to deal with the problem. The interactive exercises in particular – when you meet difficult situations and are given detailed information to work with – will be where you can demonstrate your problem-solving abilities.

Solving problems requires a systematic approach involving three main steps:

1 Gather the information you need – make sure that you cover all aspects of the problem.

2 Analyse the information – separate the relevant information from the irrelevant, then decide what is important (and what is not) and set priorities. Then identify and link causes and effects of the problem and be realistic about what can be changed and what cannot.

3 Make the decision – making sure that you take into account all the relevant factors, that you remain impartial and avoid jumping to conclusions. You should always refer to standard procedures and any useful precedents before making your decision, so make sure you use all the relevant information that you have been given.

As always there are things that you may do during the problem-solving process that will be seen as negative indicators by the assessors. A lack of attention to detail will always alert the assessors to an inability to solve problems efficiently. If you do not take the trouble to gather all the relevant facts, to identify the underlying issues and to consult other people before you reach a decision, then you are in danger of making a poor decision or making false assumptions. Some people, however, will gather too much information, much of it irrelevant, and then they are unable to analyse it efficiently. They will get stuck in the detail of complex situations and cannot see the main issues, or they will become distracted by minor issues.

Either of these approaches – too much or too little information – will reduce your chances of solving the problem effectively and will not be viewed favourably by the assessors.

Above all, your approach to the problem should be proactive and impartial.

6 PERSONAL RESPONSIBILITY

This core competency is concerned with personal qualities that a police officer must possess such as integrity, motivation, commitment, determination and conscientiousness. A good police officer will take personal responsibility for making things happen and achieving results.

Here again, a proactive approach is vital. You should show a willingness to take on tasks without having to be asked and take responsibility for your own actions. Taking the initiative is important – don't wait for others to deal with a problem – and then you must put in all the effort that is needed to get a job done. Make sure that you always meet deadlines and follow things through to a satisfactory conclusion.

The attitude you are trying to convey to the assessors is one of being open, honest and genuine, and that you are prepared to take responsibility and stand up for what is right. Personal responsibility also involves improving your own knowledge. If you have taken any steps to improve yourself recently – an evening class perhaps, or learning a language – now is the time to 'blow your own trumpet'.

Less constructive behaviour in the area of personal responsibility that the assessors will be looking out for includes giving up easily when faced with problems, putting in the minimum of effort needed to get by or not dealing with issues – just hoping that they will go away. Being unwilling to take on responsibility or blaming others rather than admitting mistakes will also be viewed negatively, as will a failure to recognise personal weaknesses and development needs.

7 RESILIENCE

Part of police work involves dealing with people in very difficult circumstances, and so applicants must be able to show that they are capable of remaining calm and confident and reaching decisions, even when the going gets tough. During the interactive exercises you will be able to show that you have the quality of resilience by remaining focused regardless of things happening around you.

As you can no doubt imagine, being able to sort out conflict and deal with hostility and provocation in a calm, non-aggressive, restrained way is an essential skill for police officers, and any opportunity that you get to demonstrate your skills in this area will be valuable. Try to show that you accept that part of the job is to make difficult decisions and that, when it is right to do so, you are prepared to stand firm despite pressure. Remaining focused and in control of situations while making and carrying through decisions and managing conflicting pressures will also be in your favour during the assessment centre.

The negative indicators that you should be aware of include showing signs of panic or agitation when you meet problems, walking away from confrontation when it would be more appropriate to get involved, getting too emotionally involved in situations, or using inappropriate physical force. As you can see, broadly speaking, the assessors will be looking for areas of inappropriate or exaggerated behaviour and, to ensure a good impression, you should moderate your reactions to difficult situations. Try not to show panic, worry or aggression.

Now let's look at the tests and exercises that make up the Selection Process.

NUMERICAL REASONING TEST

This test will check your ability to use numbers. The questions take the form of multiple-choice word problems which will test your capacity to use the maths you learned at school – the four basic arithmetical operations of addition, subtraction, division and multiplication – to work out the answers. They will involve basic calculations about measurements, money, area, time and speed (all things that you will need to understand to be a police officer) using the four basic operations plus fractions, decimals, percentages and averages. This test, consisting of 25 questions, will last for 12 minutes and you will not be allowed to use a calculator.

When carrying out the numerical reasoning test during the actual assessment, you will be required to indicate your answers by using a grid, similar to that shown below. Make sure you fill in the appropriate box in the grid completely to show, without doubt, which is your answer.

NUMERICAL REASONING ANSWER GRID

	A	B	C	D	E
1	☐	☐	☐	☐	☐
2	☐	☐	☐	☐	☐
3	☐	☐	☐	☐	☐
4	☐	☐	☐	☐	☐
5	☐	☐	☐	☐	☐

Of course, the grid you will be given in the actual test will have space for answers to 25 questions.

VERBAL LOGICAL REASONING TEST

This test is where the assessment begins to feel more like police work. You are given descriptions of situations that a police officer might meet during a shift plus some extra information about the situation. The questions take the form of conclusions that could be drawn. You are required to use logic to decide whether or not the statements about the situation are true, false or if it is impossible to say (given what you know). The situations that are described could range from a robbery or an act of vandalism to a murder or a missing person. This tests your ability to assimilate information and to reach conclusions based solely on the information that you have to hand. You should be aware here that:

- Some of the information included in the questions will have been put there to distract you and may appear to be clues to the answer, when they are not really relevant facts at all.

- You should look out for words in the statements that act as qualifiers (e.g. may, could, might have, probably and so on) as these affect the meaning of the statement.

- You may not have been told everything about the situation but you cannot assume anything.

- The statements may include reports of things that have been said. This does not mean that what has been said is necessarily true, just that it is true that that person said it.

So, you should remember that it is necessary to read every part of these questions extremely carefully.

In the same way as for the numerical reasoning test, when carrying out the verbal logical reasoning test during the actual assessment, you will be required to indicate your answers by using a grid, similar to that shown below. Again, you must ensure that you completely fill in the appropriate box in the grid to show, without doubt, which is your answer.

VERBAL LOGICAL REASONING ANSWER GRID

	A	B	C
1	☐	☐	☐
2	☐	☐	☐
3	☐	☐	☐
4	☐	☐	☐
5	☐	☐	☐

Again, the grid you will be given in the actual test will have space for answers to all the questions in that part of the test.

This test lasts for 25 minutes and consists of 31 questions.

COMPETENCY-BASED STRUCTURED INTERVIEW

During the interview, which lasts for a maximum of 20 minutes, you will be asked four questions based on how you have dealt with specific situations in the past. You are allowed up to 5 minutes to answer each question and the interviewer may ask you further questions connected with it to ensure that you answer fully and that they understand your position on the subject. All the questions are related to five of the core competencies (respect for race and diversity, teamworking, effective communication, personal responsibility and resilience) as described above.

WRITTEN EXERCISES

Here you are required to assume the role of a Customer Services Officer in a Retail and Leisure Centre, and you are given a thorough briefing about the situations before you start the written exercises. You will be required to produce a letter and a report that will be assessed for content. This includes how you have dealt with the problem posed in the exercise plus spelling and grammar, but the format or layout of the documents that you produce will not be assessed. Each of these two written exercises will last for 20 minutes.

INTERACTIVE EXERCISES

Again you will assume the role of a Customer Services Officer in a Retail and Leisure Centre. There are four interactive exercises and each of these exercises is split into two 5-minute parts – the preparation phase and the activity phase.

For the preparation phase you will be given written information about the exercise. You can study this for 5 minutes, during which time you will not be assessed.

In the activity phase you must act as a Customer Services Officer alongside role-play actors who use strict guidelines to respond to you. You must take the initiative in this phase and you are not allowed to write anything down. An assessor will also be in the room and will be making a written assessment of your performance in the exercise.

WHY ARE TESTS NECESSARY?

The varied nature of police work means that it requires a number of skills and, therefore, the recruiters must be certain that the people they choose will be able to cope well with the job. Some of the attributes that they are looking for can be discovered during interviews or physical ability tests, but others are less obvious and it is these abilities that the new Selection Process is designed to find. As mentioned previously, the new test procedures are carried out at an assessment centre, which takes approximately 5 hours. They are designed to assess each candidate holistically – to take a view of the whole person and take into account all of their qualities and capabilities, paying particular attention to the seven core competencies (see page 8).

From an employer's point of view, interviewing and taking on staff is an expensive and risky business, and the police forces of England and Wales are no exception to this. There is a number of ways in which aptitude testing can help them:

- Each police force receives a large number of applicants, and tests can whittle down the number to a more manageable and cost-effective level.

- Tests can be combined with other selection procedures to enable the employer to make better recruitment decisions.

- Tests are much less subjective than interviews alone – this is better for the employer and for the interviewees.

- Better decisions at this stage will result in fewer people leaving the force prematurely.

- Selecting the right recruits will reduce induction costs or wasted training.

- Employing the right people will lead to a reduction in the possibility of potentially dangerous or costly mistakes being made by an incompetent recruit.

- CVs are notoriously unreliable. Anyone can declare that they are numerate or literate or have an appreciation of and respect for diversity – tests will show whether or not this is actually true.

With these reasons in mind, we can see that any employer would be well advised to find a more efficient way of selecting staff than interviews alone. Mistakes in recruitment are expensive. Employers frequently use aptitude tests as an additional tool to help with their decision making – especially if they have a large number of applicants – and the National Selection Process is a set of tests designed specifically to discover the aptitudes that are desirable, or even essential, in a police officer.

HOW TO USE THIS BOOK

The tests in Chapter 2 are timed, and the answers and explanations – including tips on how to tackle the questions and some pitfalls to avoid related to the specific questions – are contained in Chapter 3. This structure allows you to test yourself in a situation as close to the actual test conditions as possible. However, as an introduction to the types of questions, we will quickly run through the whole question, answer and explanation process. Here are a few examples of the types of questions you may encounter when you sit a real test of this sort.

1 NUMERICAL REASONING TEST

Here you are given word problems to test your facility with numbers.

Solve the following problems without using a calculator.

QUESTIONS

1 A car averages 36 mph. How far will it have travelled in 4 hours?

a 144 miles

b 142 miles

c 72 miles

d 140 miles

e 74 miles

2 A person spends £68 per month on petrol. How much will he spend on petrol in a year?

  a £68

  b £800

  c £416

  d £816

  e £916

ANSWERS

1 a 144 miles

2 d £816

EXPLANATIONS

1 The answer is **a** 144 miles. Here you must multiply the average speed by the number of hours that the speed was maintained, i.e. 36 × 4 = 144. Do not let the mention of 'average speed' put you off.

2 The answer is **d** £816. This is another multiplication problem. Simply multiply the amount spent per month by the number of months in a year.

If you feel you need to refresh your knowledge of percentages, ratios and other aspects of numerical reasoning, see *Succeed at Psychometric Testing: Practice Tests for Numerical Reasoning Intermediate Level* and *Succeed at Psychometric Testing: Practice Tests for Numerical Reasoning Advanced Level* in this series.

2 VERBAL LOGICAL REASONING TEST

Here you are given descriptions of situations that a police officer may encounter plus some additional information relating to the incident. Each question is in the form of a statement about the incident and you must decide if each of these statements is true using only the evidence you have been given. You must not make assumptions or guess what the answer might be – you must use logic and reasoning to make your deductions.

You should take all the details in the description of the incident, plus the additional information given, to be true. The only decisions you need to make are about the truth – or otherwise – of the numbered statements.

Indicate your answers as follows:

Answer **A** if the statement in the question is true given the situation described and the facts that are known about it.

Answer **B** if the statement in the question is false given the situation described and the facts that are known about it.

Answer **C** if it is impossible to say whether the statement is true or false given the situation described and the facts that are known about it.

SITUATION AND QUESTIONS

At 3.30 am on Saturday 1 May, a window was smashed at Smith's Jewellers at High Street, Donfield. David Jones, landlord of the public house opposite the shop, was woken by the sound of glass smashing and witnessed a hooded man running away.

The owner of the shop was contacted at his home in Marton and arrived at 6.00 am. He reported that a ring worth £10,000 had been stolen during the raid. The following facts are also known:

- The street was deserted apart from the hooded man.
- David Jones had been drinking heavily during the evening and had gone to bed at midnight.
- As usual, the most valuable items had been removed from the jeweller's window and placed in the safe the previous evening.
- There was no evidence that anyone had entered the shop.
- A brick was found in the window.

1 A ring was stolen. ☐

2 The hooded man is a thief. ☐

3 The shop's owner does not live on the premises ☐

4 It is likely that the window was smashed with a brick. ☐

5 David Jones could have been drunk and drowsy. ☐

ANSWERS

1 B

2 C

3 A

4 A

5 A

EXPLANATIONS

1 The answer is **B**. Although the owner of the jeweller's shop has reported a ring to be stolen, we know that all valuable stock was removed from the window the previous evening and placed in the safe. We also know that no one had entered the shop so a burglary had not taken place.

2 The answer is **C**. As we have no evidence of anything having been stolen in this case, it would not necessarily be true to say that the man who broke the window is a thief, and of course just because he was seen running away does not mean that the hooded man threw the brick. However, it is not possible to say that he is definitely not a thief, so **C** is the option to choose.

3 The answer is **A**. We are told that the shop is in Donfield and the owner's home is in Marton, so it is true that he does not live on the premises.

4 The answer is **A**. The window had definitely been broken and a brick was found in the shop window.

5 The answer is **A**. We are told that David Jones had been drinking heavily so he could have been drunk. Also, as he went to bed at midnight, by 3.30 am, when the window was smashed, he would undoubtedly have been drowsy.

It should be noted here that all the people, places and incidents referred to in the verbal logical reasoning tests in this book are fictitious. Any similarity to real people, places or events is coincidental.

THE COMPETENCY-BASED STRUCTURED INTERVIEW, THE WRITTEN EXERCISES AND THE INTERACTIVE EXERCISES

As you have already seen, these parts of the assessment centre are in different formats and are therefore dealt with in a slightly different way in this book. It is not possible, as it is with the numerical reasoning test for example, to ask a straightforward question in these sections and expect to get one correct answer. The nature of the exercises determines that there will be an almost unlimited number of answers that different candidates can come up with. However, they are still well worth preparing yourself for, and some practice in thinking about your position and capabilities in the core competencies will improve your performance during the assessment centre. We have consequently included sections on these exercises giving sample questions that you can use to test yourself. There are no answers given but the explanation section will give you some guidelines on how each of the questions and exercises can be tackled. This section will also alert you to the core competencies that are likely to be assessed during each exercise and how you can bring out your best points and present yourself well.

In Chapter 4, you will find some suggestions for further improvement and some tips on how you can give your best performance on the day of the assessment centre.

NOW TRY THE TESTS

Hopefully you are now convinced that preparation, including testing yourself using the tests in this book, will definitely improve your performance – and your chances of getting into the police force of your choice. So, on with the tests.

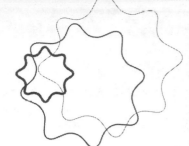

CHAPTER 2
TIMED TESTS

NUMERICAL REASONING
TEST 1

(Answers to this test can be found on pages 131–133.)

Solve the following problems without using a calculator.
Allow yourself 12 minutes.

1 If a family spends £112 per month on running its car, how
much would it cost for the year?

a £144

b £1344

c £1120

d £1340

e £1240

2 A policeman walks 9 miles a day. If he works 5 days per
week, how far would he have walked after 6 weeks?

a 250 miles

b 54 miles

c 30 miles

d 45 miles

e 270 miles

3 A call from a mobile phone lasts 12 minutes. If the first minute costs 30p and all other time is charged at 5p per minute, how much did the call cost?

a £1.30

b £8.50

c £0.85

d £0.30

e £0.55

4 If a train journey usually takes 1 hour 35 minutes, but stops for 45 minutes, how long would this journey take?

a 2 hours 20 minutes

b 180 minutes

c 2 hours 10 minutes

d 160 minutes

e 3 hours 20 minutes

5 A bill at the DIY store comes to £48. How much would you have to pay if you are given a 10% discount?

a £45.20

b £43.20

c £44

d £45

e £43

6 A coach carrying 47 passengers crashes and 18 of them are injured. How many are not injured?

a 26

b 27

c 28

d 29

e 30

7 The food bill for a party is £85.50, £63 is spent on drink and £27 on CDs. What is the total spent?

a £175.50

b £175

c £148.50

d £180

e £185.50

8 Ninety-six people attend a conference. Two-thirds of them are non-smokers. How many people are smokers at the conference?

a 64

b 32

c 33

d 45

e 35

9 A van contains five boxes weighing 93 kg in total plus six parcels weighing 12 kg each. What is the total weight of the van's load?

a 537 kg

b 105 kg

c 153 kg

d 165 kg

e 160 kg

10 What is the average weight of a group of people if one weighs 61 kg, one is 65 kg, two are 70 kg and two are 77 kg?

a 67 kg

b 69 kg

c 75 kg

d 70 kg

e 65 kg

11 If a motorist is travelling at 85 mph in a road where the speed limit is 60 mph, by how much is he exceeding the limit?

a 15 mph

b 20 mph

c 25 mph

d 30 mph

e 10 mph

12 How much does it cost to buy six tins of paint at £15.50 each?

  a £93

  b £95

  c £96

  d £92.50

  e £90

13 If a clerk works 8 hours per day from Monday to Thursday but only 5 hours on Friday, how many hours will he work in a week?

  a 35

  b 36

  c 37

  d 38

  e 39

14 A floor takes 180 tiles. If a woman buys 20 boxes of 12 tiles, how many boxes will she have left over?

  a 0

  b 12

  c 60

  d 4

  e 5

15 If it has been calculated that 250 officers walked a total of 50,000 miles, how many miles would they each have walked on average?

  a 250

  b 200

  c 500

  d 100

  e 1000

16 Eighty-four vehicles are stopped in a traffic survey. If every third vehicle was stopped for the survey, how many vehicles were there altogether?

  a 84

  b 200

  c 28

  d 252

  e 250

17 If your quarterly phone bill is £72.24, how much have you spent per month on average?

  a £24

  b £24.08

  c £288.96

  d £18.06

  e £26.08

18 A mother has three pies to share between her four
children. If the eldest has a full pie and the next two have
$^3/_4$ each, how much is left for the youngest child?

a None

b $^1/_4$

c $^1/_2$

d $^3/_4$

e 1

19 Two hundred chairs are set out for a conference. If 180
people attended, what percentage of chairs would not be
used?

a 20%

b 7%

c 5%

d 15%

e 10%

20 When paying a bill in cash, you give the shopkeeper four
£10 notes and one £20 note and receive three £1 coins in
change. How much did you pay?

a £57

b £67

c £47

d £60

e £3

21 You have two boxes of paper containing five reams each. How many sheets of paper do you have? NB: One ream = 250 sheets.

a 1250

b 1000

c 5000

d 2000

e 2500

22 If a CD contains tracks lasting 32 minutes in total, how many times could you play it in 12 hours 16 minutes?

a 12

b 23

c 22

d 24

e 32

23 If it costs 8p per unit of electricity and an electric heater uses 15 units per hour, how much would it cost to run the heater for 3 hours?

a £1.20

b £2.40

c £3.60

d £3.50

e £3

24 Two people buy theatre tickets at £22 each, a meal costing £8 each and then share a taxi at £24. How much did they spend in total?

  a £88

  b £80

  c £54

  d £108

  e £84

25 A room is 3 m by 3.5 m. How many metres of carpet, 3 m wide, would you need?

  a 2 m

  b 2.5 m

  c 3 m

  d 3.5 m

  e 4 m

TEST 2

(Answers to this test can be found on pages 134–136.)

Solve the following problems without using a calculator. Allow yourself 12 minutes.

1 A cake contains ½ kg each of currants and sultanas and 125 gms each of mixed peel and cherries. How much fruit is this in total?

   a 750 gms

   b 1 kg 250 gms

   c 1½ kilos

   d 1000 gms

   e 1 kg 500 gms

2 If a worker earns £250 per week and then receives a 5% pay rise, how much would her new wage be?

   a £255.50

   b £255

   c £265

   d £262

   e £262.50

3 You receive a 12% discount on a bill of £150. How much did you have to pay?

a £132.50

b £130

c £132

d £128

e £126

4 If three office workers start at 9 am and finish at 5 pm with an hour for lunch, how long will they have worked between them in 5 days?

a 105 hours

b 110 hours

c 35 hours

d 40 hours

e 37 hours

5 You cancel your holiday and must lose your 5% deposit. If the cost of the holiday for your family was £1080, how much will you lose?

a £108

b £56

c £58

d £54

e £66

6 One sixth of a company's 102 workers are temporary. How many workers are permanent?

a 90

b 85

c 80

d 75

e 70

7 One bottle of wine costs £4.99. How much will a dozen bottles cost if there is a 10% discount on all orders of ten or more bottles?

a £56

b £55

c £59.88

d £53.95

e £53.89

8 At 83p per litre, how much would it cost to fill a fuel tank with a capacity of 60 litres?

a £49.80

b £50

c £47.80

d £48.90

e £49

9 A patio is 3 m wide and 4 m long. How many paving bricks would it take if there are 32 in a square metre?

a 388

b 386

c 384

d 584

e 484

10 A plane ticket costs £189 plus £11.50 tax. If you took a taxi to the airport at a cost of £15, how much would your journey have cost?

a £204

b £180.50

c £200.50

d £215.50

e £115.50

11 After a robbery only £14.63 was left in the till. If there had been £112 before the theft, how much had been stolen?

a £87.67

b £87.37

c £79.37

d £97.37

e £97.67

12 A website has 490 hits per day. How many in a week?

   a 2480

   b 3480

   c 2430

   d 2450

   e 3430

13 A box contained 144 pens. If one third of them are taken, how many are left?

   a 98

   b 38

   c 94

   d 48

   e 96

14 If a train leaves at 9.30 am and arrives at 2.45 in the afternoon, how long has the journey taken?

   a 5 hours 15 minutes

   b 6 hours 15 minutes

   c 4 hours 25 minutes

   d 4 hours 15 minutes

   e 5 hours 25 minutes

15 How much would be left after cutting four curtains at 1.35 m each from a piece of fabric 6 m long?

  a 2.7 m

  b 5.4 m

  c 0.65 m

  d 1.6 m

  e 0.6 m

16 If four police officers make an average of four arrests each per day, how many arrests would be made in total in a week?

  a 112

  b 116

  c 108

  d 120

  e 56

17 If a motorist travels at an average speed of 30 mph and lives 20 miles from work, how long would it take her to drive to work?

  a 20 minutes

  b 1 hour

  c 40 minutes

  d 30 minutes

  e 50 minutes

18 What is the average number of hits per hour if a website gets 3852 hits in 12 hours?

a 231

b 321

c 280

d 320

e 32

19 If a room takes 2.75 litres to paint each coat and the decorator gives it three coats of paint, how much paint will he need?

a 7.25 litres

b 7.5 litres

c 7.75 litres

d 8 litres

e 8.25 litres

20 Eighty-one items are removed from a scene of crime. If only two thirds are deemed relevant and the remainder discarded, how many are discarded?

a 27

b 9

c 37

d 54

e 21

21 If one removal van can carry 23 items of furniture on average, how many vans would be needed to move 184 items?

a 23

b 5

c 6

d 7

e 8

22 A survey found that three quarters of homeowners do not belong to a neighbourhood watch scheme. In a town of 5000 houses, how many would not belong to such a scheme?

a 1250

b 1500

c 2250

d 3750

e 4000

23 Materials for landscaping a garden cost £535. If the turf costs £120, the concrete costs £35 and the paving slabs cost £203, how much is left for the plants?

a £77

b £177

c £277

d £203

e £183

24 The average temperature over 3 days was 68°F. If the temperature was 64 on the first day and 66 on the second, what was the temperature on the third day?

a 70°F

b 72°F

c 74°F

d 68°F

e 76°F

25 What percentage of cash has been stolen if there was £800 before the robbery and only £80 left after the robbery?

a 10%

b 40%

c 60%

d 80%

e 90%

TEST 3

(Answers to this test can be found on pages 136–140.)

Solve the following problems without using a calculator. Allow yourself 12 minutes.

1 If one box of pens costs £4.99, how much would a package of five boxes cost?

a £20

b £24.95

c £25.95

d £19.99

e £39.90

2 An office stationery invoice is made up of £26.30 for envelopes, £14.25 for pens and pencils and £93.00 for printer cartridges plus £23.37 VAT. What would be the total invoice amount?

a £133.55

b £157.02

c £157.92

d £156.02

e £156.92

3 Eight people work in your section with an average salary of £25,000. What would be the total annual salaries?

a £200,000

b £115,000

c £120,000

d £3125

e £225,000

4 A force's weekly overtime bill is £1500. If each of the 20 members of staff has earned an equal share of this, how much will each receive?

a £75

b £7.50

c £95

d £15

e £150

5 If each member of the workforce of 15 people works 4.5 hours overtime in a week, how much overtime in total will have been worked?

a 20 hours

b 47.5 hours

c 40 hours

d 30 hours

e 67.5 hours

6 Only a quarter of all the applicants for a police entry exam are over 25 years old. If 224 people applied, how many are over 25?

a 168

b 50

c 58

d 56

e 65

7 Of 880 employees, 20% are office based. How many is this?

a 176

b 180

c 220

d 440

e 156

8 If a worker earns £220 per week and is then given a 5% increase, what will the new weekly wage be?

a £231

b £230

c £225

d £240.50

e £250

9 If nine out of ten workers drive to work, what percentage of workers do not drive to work?

a 9%

b 10%

c 50%

d 25%

e 90%

10 A fifth of a force's constables have received firearms training. If there are 100 constables in total, how many have not received any training?

a 40

b 20

c 80

d 50

e 60

11 Three quarters of a force's staff eat in the canteen. If there are 208 members of staff, how many do not eat in the canteen?

a 56

b 156

c 48

d 50

e 52

12 If six friends go together to a restaurant and spend an average of £20.50 each, then share the bill equally between them, how much would they each have to pay?

   a £20

   b £20.50

   c £21.50

   d £41

   e £123

13 If your restaurant bill comes to £67.50 and you decide to add a 10% tip, how much would you pay in total?

   a £77.50

   b £74.25

   c £75

   d £73

   e £72.25

14 A printer produces eight pages per minute. How long – in hours and minutes – would ten copies of a document consisting of 76 pages take to print?

   a 1 hour 35 minutes

   b 3 hours 10 minutes

   c 95 minutes

   d 304 minutes

   e 76 minutes

15 If the cost of 9000 items is £3519, what is the cost of each item?

a £4.91

b £3.91

c £0.391

d £0.39

e £0.04

16 Four police officers take 1½ hours in total to assemble items of evidence. If only one officer was doing this job, how many hours would it take her?

a 5 hours

b 4 hours

c 6 hours

d 1½ hours

e 10 hours

17 If rail ticket prices go up by 5%, how much would the new price of a ticket be if it costs £90 before the increase?

a £94.50

b £100

c £99

d £4.50

e £92.50

18 A third of a police section's 210 employees are selected for special training. How many is this?

a 21

b 140

c 80

d 70

e 60

19 Half of a company's invoices are paid on time and a third are paid a month late. The remainder is still outstanding. Of a total invoice value of £360,000, what is the value of the invoices that have been paid?

a £25,000

b £250,000

c £30,000

d £36,000

e £300,000

20 Only one in ten members of a police force have been with the force for over 10 years. If 50% have been with the force less than 1 year, what percentage have been there between 1 and 10 years?

a 60%

b 40%

c 10%

d 25%

e 50%

21 A pair of sunglasses, which originally cost £25, has been reduced in the sale by 12%. What is the sale price?

  a £22

  b £20

  c £22.50

  d £15

  e £17.50

22 If I go on duty at 6 am and finish the shift at 3 pm, how many hours will I have worked after 5 days?

  a 35 hours

  b 37 hours

  c 39 hours

  d 40 hours

  e 45 hours

23 If two accidents occur every week on average on a particularly dangerous stretch of road, how many accidents, on average, will occur in 28 days?

  a 6

  b 8

  c 10

  d 12

  e 14

24 A man is fined £124.50 including costs. This is equivalent to a third of his take home pay each week. How much is his take home pay?

a £375

b £275.50

c £325.50

d £373.50

e £353.50

25 If you negotiate a 5% discount on a car with a list price of £14,500, how much will you have to pay?

a £13,775

b £13,500

c £13,050

d £14,000

e £14,250

TEST 4

(Answers to this test can be found on pages 140–143.)

Solve the following without using a calculator. Allow yourself 12 minutes.

1 Five friends go together to a restaurant and spend a total of £127.50. If they then share the bill equally between them, how much would they each have to pay?

   a £30

   b £25.50

   c £25

   d £51

   e £127.50

2 If your taxi fare comes to £17.50 and you decide to add a 10% tip, how much would you pay in total?

   a £19.25

   b £22

   c £17.50

   d £15.75

   e £19.50

3 A printer produces eight pages per minute. How long – in hours and minutes – would ten copies of a document consisting of 64 pages take to print?

a 10 hours 40 minutes

b 3 hours 10 minutes

c 1 hour 20 minutes

d 80 minutes

e 76 minutes

4 If the cost of 5000 items is £1100, what is the cost of each item?

a £0.44

b £22

c £2.20

d £0.22

e £0.022

5 If there is a 15% discount on an order for 200 shirts at £10 each, how much would the total order cost?

a £1700

b £1750

c £1000

d £1650

e £1400

6 Six workers take 2 hours in total to pack an order. If only one worker was doing this job, how long would it take her?

a 6 hours

b 4 hours

c 12 hours

d 1½ hours

e 10 hours

7 A worker produces 227 items but nine are rejected. How many are accepted?

a 217

b 219

c 227

d 218

e 236

8 If rail ticket prices go up by 5%, how much would the new price of a ticket be if it costs £60 before the increase?

a £62.50

b £57.50

c £70

d £65

e £63

9 A third of a company's 90 employees are members of their healthcare scheme. How many is this?

a 30

b 40

c 80

d 70

e 60

10 A police force surveys its constables and finds that 60% are in favour of a new scheme while a further 15% are against. The remainder did not respond to the survey. Of 400 constables, how many did not respond?

a 240

b 100

c 60

d 300

e 125

11 Fifty per cent of a company's workers are below average height. If the company employs 126 people, how many are shorter than average?

a 120

b 100

c 63

d 65

e 73

12 If a production department manufactures 5000 machine parts but only 80% are of the required quality, how many have to be rejected?

a 800

b 1000

c 4000

d 3000

e 500

13 A survey of a company's 246 customers shows that a third of them are unlikely to place further orders with the company. How many is this?

a 140

b 100

c 164

d 82

e 92

14 A modification to your printer results in a 10% reduction in printing time. If 120 pages took 10 minutes prior to the modification, how long would it now take to print 120 pages?

a 9 minutes

b $8\frac{1}{2}$ minutes

c 10 minutes

d 11 minutes

e 8 minutes

15 If one desk costs £150 but a discount of 10% is available if you buy two, how much would two desks cost in total?

a £240

b £300

c £270

d £290

e £285

16 A supplier reduces all her prices by 12½%. How much would your usual monthly order of £800 cost after this reduction?

a £730

b £800

c £600

d £750

e £700

17 Seventy-five per cent of a company's employees are female. Of a total workforce of 1540 how many are male?

a 240

b 385

c 360

d 1155

e 770

18 If you work 8 out of 24 hours, what fraction of the day do you work?

a ½

b One third

c ¼

d One sixth

e Two thirds

19 Twelve boxes of spare parts weigh 240 kg. How much do three boxes weigh?

a 20 kg

b 40 kg

c 60 kg

d 30 kg

e 80 kg

20 A collection for a colleague's retirement gift yields £180. If there are 30 members of staff, what was the average contribution?

a £7

b £6

c £5

d £3

e £4

21 A police force spends an average of £95 per month on catering. How much would their annual catering bill be?

a £1200

b £1150

c £1135

d £1140

e £950

22 The cost of a plane ticket to Paris was £95 plus tax of £15. If your taxi to the airport was £13, how much did the journey cost in total?

a £113

b £110

c £118

d £125

e £123

23 A company has sales of £105,000. If the wholesale cost of the goods was £50,000 and delivery charges totalled £2500, how much profit did they make?

a £52,500

b £50,000

c £52,000

d £42,500

e £62,500

24 A man is 8 kg heavier than his son who weighs 97 kg. How heavy is the man?

   a 99 kg

   b 89 kg

   c 105 kg

   d 100 kg

   e 108 kg

25 A woman works for 3½ hours then takes a break of 1 hour. She then works for a further 4 hours and drives for 30 minutes to get home. How long did she spend working?

   a 8½ hrs

   b 7½ hrs

   c 7¼ hrs

   d 9 hrs

   e 6½ hrs

TEST 5

(Answers to this test can be found on pages 143–145.)

Solve the following without using a calculator. Allow yourself 12 minutes.

1 If a man has served 40% of a 10-year sentence, how long has he got left to serve?

a 5 years

b 5 years 6 months

c 6 years

d 6 years 6 months

e 4 years

2 If a burglar enters three houses in a street of 12 houses, what fraction of the houses has she entered?

a $\frac{1}{4}$

b 25%

c One-third

d $\frac{1}{2}$

e 33%

3 A train journey is scheduled to take $2\frac{1}{2}$ hours but is delayed by 10 minutes. What time would the train arrive if it left at 08.34?

a 11.24

b 10.14

c 11.04

d 10.56

e 11.14

4 Traffic offences in a particular area are reduced by 15%. If there were previously 200 offences, how many were there after the reduction?

a 150

b 170

c 165

d 160

e 175

5 If seven out of 20 cars on a car park do not display a valid road tax disc, what percentage is this?

a 40%

b 35%

c 45%

d 33%

e 30%

6 If three men worked 2 hours each at £9 per hour, what would the wages bill be?

a £55

b £63

c £50

d £54

e £45

7 A journey takes 5 hours 15 minutes by car but only 2 hours 40 minutes by train. How much quicker is the train?

a 1 hour 35 minutes

b 2 hours 45 minutes

c 3 hours 35 minutes

d 2 hours 15 minutes

e 2 hours 35 minutes

8 If you buy a sandwich at £1.99, a drink at £1.15 and a bar of chocolate at 80p, how much have you spent?

a £4

b £3.84

c £3.94

d £4.94

e £2.96

9 The cost of your car insurance rises by 15%. If the cost was £305 before the increase, how much is the new cost?

a £350

b £45.75

c £350.75

d £405.70

e £355

10 Two hundred trees were planted by an estate manager but 25 died. What fraction of the trees did this loss represent?

a $\frac{1}{8}$

b $\frac{1}{2}$

c $\frac{1}{6}$

d 25%

e $12\frac{1}{2}$%

11 If 25% of stolen goods were returned following a burglary, what fraction was not returned?

a 75%

b $\frac{1}{2}$

c $\frac{1}{4}$

d $\frac{3}{4}$

e 25%

12 If a company's IT department has 14 PCs and 12 printers, how many of each will be left if 50% are stolen?

a 6 PCs, 7 printers

b 6 PCs, 6 printers

c 7 PCs, 6 printers

d 8 PCs, 6 printers

e 6 PCs, 4 printers

13 If a till contained £353.53 before a robbery during which all the paper money amounting to £325 was stolen, how much did the till contain in coins?

a £28.53

b £25.53

c £50.52

d £25.35

e £30.53

14 If you walk for 2½ hours at 4 mph, how far will you have walked?

a 8½ miles

b 8 miles

c 10½ miles

d 10 miles

e 12 miles

15 If you buy two train tickets at £45.90 each, pay £5 for parking at the station and £61 for a hotel room, how much will you have spent?

a £157.80

b £159

c £160

d £156.80

e £157.90

16 If one shopping bag contains eight cans of food weighing 0.5 kg each and another bag contains two 1-kg bags of sugar, how much heavier is one bag than the other?

a 6 kg

b 1 kg

c 8 kg

d 4 kg

e 2 kg

17 If a police officer's shoes last, on average, 4 months, how many pairs of shoes would she need in a 22-year career?

a 44 pairs

b 66 pairs

c 22 pairs

d 40 pairs

e 60 pairs

18 A man swims 15 lengths of a 25-m long pool. How far has he swum in total?

  a 425 m

  b 325 m

  c 375 m

  d 350 m

  e 475 m

19 If you buy ten CDs at £12 each and then receive a discount of 5%, how much would you pay in total?

  a £110

  b £11.40

  c £125

  d £114

  e £120

20 If street lights in a shopping area are automatically switched on from 8 am to 10 pm, what fraction of each day are the lights off?

  a $\frac{1}{2}$

  b $\frac{5}{12}$

  c $\frac{7}{12}$

  d $\frac{1}{3}$

  e $\frac{1}{4}$

21 If 95% of a hotel's bedrooms are occupied and the remaining six rooms are not, how many rooms does the hotel have in total?

a 126 rooms

b 110 rooms

c 114 rooms

d 100 rooms

e 120 rooms

22 If it takes three police officers 2 days to complete an investigation, how many officers would be needed to get the job done in half a day?

a 6

b 4

c 3

d 10

e 12

23 A fuel tank holds 50 litres. If it already contains 45 litres, how much would it cost to fill it up if fuel costs £0.81 per litre?

a £5.05

b £4.05

c £3.50

d £45

e £40.50

24 What is the average width of five gardens in a street if the widths are 10 m, 12 m, 12.5 m, 10.5 m and 15 m?

a 12 m

b 10 m

c 11 m

d 11.5 m

e 12.5 m

25 Twenty-five per cent of 64 people in a public house are female. How many are male?

a 24

b 48

c 39

d 40

e 35

TEST 6

(Answers to this test can be found on pages 145–148.)

Solve the following without using a calculator. Allow yourself 12 minutes.

1 If you buy several items in a supermarket totalling £12.76, how much change would you be given if you paid with a £20 note?

a £7.24

b £7.34

c £8.24

d £8.34

e £8.14

2 Of a group of eight women, six have blonde hair. What percentage do not have blonde hair?

a 30%

b 33%

c 15%

d 25%

e 20%

3 If two chairs weigh 17 kg, how much do eight chairs weigh?

a 136 kg

b 117 kg

c 68 kg

d 86 kg

e 66 kg

4 In a bag containing 21 sweets, seven were found to be broken. What fraction was broken?

a ½

b ⅓

c ¼

d ⅔

e ⅙

5 A businesswoman travels 180 miles in 4 hours. What was the average speed of her journey?

a 60 mph

b 35 mph

c 40 mph

d 50 mph

e 45 mph

6 Four books contain 192 pages each and two more have 124 pages each. How many pages in total?

a 1106

b 1082

c 1632

d 1016

e 892

7 If it takes an average of 1 hour 13 minutes to travel to work and 1 hour 10 minutes to come back, how much time would be spent travelling in 5 days?

a 11 hours 55 minutes

b 10 hours 55 minutes

c 12 hours

d 2 hours 23 minutes

e 6 hours 5 minutes

8 If each cinema ticket costs £4.50 and the takings from one showing are £567, how many people watched the film?

a 135

b 126

c 150

d 120

e 130

9 If a family spends £63 on food each week, how much will it have spent in 6 weeks?

a £276

b £278

c £376

d £378

e £380

10 A man works 2 hours overtime after his usual working day of 8 hours. If he starts at 8.30 am and takes 1 hour for lunch, what time would he finish?

a 7.30 pm

b 8.30 pm

c 7.30 am

d 6.30 pm

e 7.00 pm

11 What is the average height of a group of people if three are 1.59 m, two are 1.6 m and two are 1.79 m?

a 1.59 m

b 1.65 m

c 1.92 m

d 1.6 m

e 1.79 m

12 If a car is travelling at an average speed of 48 mph, how far will it have travelled in 15 minutes?

a 10 miles

b 15 miles

c 12 miles

d 48 miles

e 24 miles

13 Eight CDs at a total cost of £79.92 were purchased. If they all cost the same, how much did one CD cost?

a £12.99

b £8.99

c £9.50

d £9.99

e £10.99

14 If a delivery van contains 20 parcels each weighing 6.5 kg, how much would its cargo weigh after five of the parcels had been delivered?

a 100 kg

b 97.5 kg

c 130 kg

d 32.5 kg

e 87.5 kg

15 If you earn £25,000 per annum and then receive a 3% pay increase, how much would your new salary be?

a £25,500

b £25,950

c £25,350

d £25,300

e £25,750

16 If a decorator has 75 litres of paint, how many rooms can she paint if each room takes 12.5 litres?

a 12

b 6

c 9

d 5

e 2

17 If a 3-minute phone call to China costs £1.05, how much would a 15-minute call cost?

a £5.50

b £4.75

c £5

d £5.25

e £4.50

18 A case of wine costs £60 and contains 12 bottles. How much will four bottles cost?

a £25

b £40

c £15

d £30

e £20

19 A car's fuel tank has a maximum capacity of 60 litres. If it already contains 23 litres, how many more will be required to fill it?

a 37 litres

b 40 litres

c 27 litres

d 47 litres

e 43 litres

20 A family spends an average of £54 weekly on food. How much will its annual food bill be?

a £5400

b £2808

c £280.80

d £2800

e £2600

21 If you select goods to the value of £29.60 in the supermarket but only have £18.45 in your pocket, how much short of what you need will you be?

a £11.45

b £15.15

c £13.25

d £11.15

e £10.15

22 If I go to yoga classes lasting 40 minutes twice a week and aerobics classes lasting 30 minutes each three times a week, how long will I have spent in exercise classes?

a 3 hours

b 2 hours 30 minutes

c 1 hour 50 minutes

d 2 hours 50 minutes

e 3 hours 50 minutes

23 If you pay for six theatre tickets at £18 each and there Is a booking fee of £1.50 per ticket, how much would it cost you in total?

a £118

b £108

c £117

d £127.50

e £120

24 If a police constable goes on duty at 08.00 and finishes her shift at 16.30, how long will she have worked after 3 days?

a 26 hours

b 25 hours

c 25½ hours

d 24½ hours

e 24 hours

25 If a taped interview lasted 20 minutes, what fraction of a 90-minute tape will have been used?

a ²⁄₉

b ⅓

c ¼

d ⅕

e ⅑

VERBAL LOGICAL REASONING

TEST 1

(Answers to this test can be found on pages 148–151.)

Here you are given descriptions of situations that a police officer may encounter plus some additional information relating to the incident. Each question is in the form of a statement about the incident and you must decide if it is true using only the evidence you have been given. You should take all the details in the description of the incident, plus the additional information given, to be true. The only decisions you need to make are about the truth – or otherwise – of the numbered statements.

Indicate your answers as follows:

Answer **A** if the statement in the question is true given the situation described and the facts that are known about it.

Answer **B** if the statement in the question is false given the situation described and the facts that are known about it.

Answer **C** if it is impossible to say whether the statement is true or false given the situation described and the facts that are known about it.

Allow yourself 25 minutes.

At 8.30 am two children received minor injuries when a car hit them on a zebra crossing while they were on their way to school. The car did not stop. Later the same day a red sports car was found abandoned in the town. The following facts are also known:

- No one saw the accident but a red car was reported being driven recklessly in a nearby street at 8.35 am.

- At 6 am the owner of the red car reported it stolen from his drive.

- The children were aged 7 and 9.

- The children were not accompanied by an adult.

1 The driver stopped after the accident. ☐

2 The red car injured the children. ☐

3 The red car was stolen. ☐

4 The two children attended the same school. ☐

5 The children were on their way home. ☐

A number of thefts from garden sheds were reported in Middletown during August but the police have no leads as to who is responsible.

On 16 September, Peter Cornwell reported the theft of a lawnmower from his garden in nearby Farnham. It is also known that:

- Peter Cornwell had two lawnmowers.
- Nothing worth more than £5 was stolen from the garden sheds.
- Several youths had been trespassing in gardens in Middletown.
- The police do not believe the incidents in Middletown are connected to the theft in Farnham.

6 Recently recovered goods can now be returned to their owners. ☐

7 Peter Cornwell will make an insurance claim for his stolen lawnmower. ☐

8 Several expensive items of equipment were stolen from the sheds. ☐

9 The youths broke into the sheds. ☐

10 The thefts from the sheds occurred in August. ☐

A large supermarket was cleared of customers after the manager had received a phone call warning him that there was a bomb in the store. Business resumed the following day after a complete search, when nothing suspicious was found. It is also known that:

- Two employees had been sacked the previous week for theft.
- There were several unidentified cartons found in the storeroom.
- The unidentified cartons were found to contain redundant stock.
- It was a fine day and the shop workers were sent home.
- The store man had a reputation for being careless.

11 One (or both) of the sacked employees held a grudge against the company. ☐

12 The store man caused the scare. ☐

13 The shop workers were happy to be sent home. ☐

14 The telephone call was a hoax. ☐

15 The bomb was hidden in the store. ☐

The body of a middle-aged man was found in a burnt-out car on waste ground in a run-down area of the city. There was no one else in the car. The following information is also known:

- The fire brigade was frequently called to the waste ground to deal with burning cars.

- An 18-year-old drug addict was also a frequent visitor to the area and has been reported missing since the fire.

- The inquest and post mortem found that the man died from smoke inhalation.

- A piece of pipe was found alongside the car.

- Children frequently played on the land.

16 The man committed suicide. ☐

17 The drug addict died in the fire. ☐

18 The children could have set fire to the car. ☐

19 The effects of the fire killed the man. ☐

20 Drug addicts were common in the area. ☐

A 6-week-old baby girl was found dead by her mother when she went to get her from her cot on the morning of Friday 4 September. The woman's elder daughter called an ambulance and the police. The following facts are also known:

- A neighbour reported that the baby was often left alone in the house.
- The NSPCC had visited the family twice prior to the baby's death.
- The police told the mother that the death would be treated as suspicious and would therefore have to be investigated.
- The woman's ex-husband had not had any contact with her for over 2 years.

21 The baby was the woman's only child. ☐

22 The baby was born in the summer. ☐

23 This was a 'cot death'. ☐

24 The neighbour had called the NSPCC. ☐

25 The mother killed the baby. ☐

Several shopkeepers in the village of Barchester had money taken from them by people posing as tax inspectors. Six shops in just one street had been targeted by the team. The following is also known:

- Two shopkeepers reported visits from 'suspicious characters' but had not had money stolen.

- The local tax office confirmed that they would not visit without appointments.

- During the investigation it was found out that the owner of the local fish and chip shop had been keeping false records of his takings.

- Sylvia Marks, the owner of a dress shop in Barchester, reported that she thought she recognised one of the thieves.

26 All the thieves were men. ☐

27 All the shopkeepers were women. ☐

28 The people posing as tax inspectors were not always successful in obtaining money. ☐

29 The team targeted a local area. ☐

30 The shopkeepers were trying to avoid paying tax. ☐

31 All the shopkeepers who lost money will make insurance claims to recover their losses. ☐

TEST 2

(Answers to this test can be found on pages 151–154.)

Here you are given descriptions of situations that a police officer may encounter plus some additional information relating to the incident. Each question is in the form of a statement about the incident and you must decide if it is true using only the evidence you have been given. You should take all the details in the description of the incident, plus the additional information given, to be true. The only decisions you need to make are about the truth – or otherwise – of the numbered statements.

Indicate your answers as follows:

Answer **A** if the statement in the question is true given the situation described and the facts that are known about it.

Answer **B** if the statement in the question is false given the situation described and the facts that are known about it.

Answer **C** if it is impossible to say whether the statement is true or false given the situation described and the facts that are known about it.

Allow yourself 25 minutes.

Paul Brookes, aged 14, was arrested at his father's home on Wednesday 9 July on suspicion of taking a car without the owner's consent on the previous day. He denied the charges and said he had been at school at the time in question. The following information has also been ascertained:

- When informed of the arrest, Paul's mother insisted that he could not drive.
- The Head Teacher of Paul's school confirmed that Paul had been absent from school on both Tuesday 8 and Wednesday 9 July.
- Paul had been cautioned for shoplifting when he was 11.
- Paul's mother and father are divorced.
- Paul's father admitted that he had allowed Paul to drive his car on a field at the rear of his house.
- The Head Teacher referred to Paul as a bright but disturbed child.

1 This is Paul's first alleged offence. ☐

2 Paul tells lies to get himself out of trouble. ☐

3 Paul's parents have no contact with each other. ☐

4 Paul cannot drive so he must be innocent. ☐

5 Paul is frequently absent from school. ☐

Molly Smith, aged 5, was kidnapped from outside her school at 3.30 pm on Tuesday 21 June as she waited for her sister Katie, aged 10. The two girls are usually collected by their mother. The following is also known:

- The school caretaker saw Katie at 3.45 pm.

- It is the school's policy not to allow children under 8 to leave school unless accompanied by a parent.

- Molly's regular teacher was off sick and had been replaced this week by a temporary teacher.

- When interviewed the teacher stated that Molly's mother had collected her.

- A tall woman was seen talking to Molly as she waited.

- Molly's mother is short and overweight.

6 The school has not carried out its duties adequately. ☐

7 Molly was collected by her mother. ☐

8 Katie was late meeting her sister. ☐

9 The two girls are good friends. ☐

10 The caretaker is responsible for ensuring that all children are collected. ☐

Two neighbours – Stuart, aged 10 and Terry, aged 11 – were reported missing by their mothers late in the evening of Friday 6 August. Neither of them have been seen since they called at Terry's home for a snack after school. It is also known that:

- Neither boy has ever been in trouble with the police.
- Stuart's mother works part-time in a shop.
- Terry had complained of bullying at school.
- Stuart has a mobile phone but there was no reply when the police tried to contact him.
- Stuart's mother and father are divorced.
- Both boys' bikes are also missing.

11 The boys have gone for a bike ride. ☐

12 The boys have run away because of the bullying. ☐

13 Terry had been bullied by Stuart. ☐

14 The two boys lived close to one another. ☐

15 Terry is an orphan. ☐

Carl McCartney was severely injured in a car crash at 10.30 am on Thursday 7 June. He was taken to Middletown General Hospital where he was admitted to the Intensive Care Unit. By coincidence, this is the hospital where Carl works. It is also known that:

- Two cars were involved in the collision.

- There were no witnesses.

- The other driver was only slightly injured and refused to be taken to hospital.

- Carl had taken delivery of his new car earlier that morning.

- The other driver said she had seen a dog run in front of Carl's car immediately before the collision.

16 Carl was unfamiliar with his car. ☐

17 The other driver was a woman. ☐

18 Carl is a doctor. ☐

19 The other driver was not injured severely enough to warrant hospital treatment. ☐

20 The accident was caused by careless driving. ☐

A 36-year-old man has been arrested on suspicion of the assault of an elderly couple outside their home in Ash Street, Northtown. Shortly before midnight the couple, Mary and Cyril Jones, were returning to their home after a night out on Friday 16 June when they were attacked by James Barnes as they got out of their car. The following is also known:

- Mary and Cyril were both 72.

- The thief stole Mary's purse and Cyril's wallet.

- James Barnes cannot drive.

- Mary and Cyril had never met their attacker before.

- James Barnes had received a visit from a bailiff earlier that day.

21 There was no motive for the attack. ☐

22 James Barnes was outside Mary and Cyril's house when they arrived home. ☐

23 The attack was pre-planned. ☐

24 James Barnes had no money problems. ☐

25 After the attack, the elderly couple both suffered severe shock. ☐

A block of flats was partially destroyed by an explosion on Monday 14 July. Reliable witnesses reported seeing a short, elderly man hurrying from the block's front entrance shortly before the explosion. It is also known that:

- The smell of gas had been reported to the Gas Board the previous week.
- Tom Cross, aged 63, was the building's caretaker.
- The police are investigating the possible terrorist connections of one of the building's tenants.
- Tom Cross is 6ft 3inches tall.
- The caretaker was due to take early retirement the following week.
- A senior politician lived in one of the flats.

26 The gas leak caused the explosion. ☐

27 Terrorists targeted the politician. ☐

28 Tom Cross could not have been responsible for the explosion. ☐

29 The caretaker was the man seen leaving the flats in a hurry. ☐

30 Explosives were found in one of the flats. ☐

31 The Gas Board will be held responsible. ☐

TEST 3

(Answers to this test can be found on pages 154–156.)

Here you are given descriptions of situations that a police officer may encounter plus some additional information relating to the incident. Each question is then in the form of a statement about the incident and you must decide if it is true using only the evidence you have been given. You should take all the details in the description of the incident, plus the additional information given, to be true. The only decisions you need to make are about the truth – or otherwise – of the numbered statements.

Indicate your answers as follows:

Answer **A** if the statement in the question is true given the situation described and the facts that are known about it.

Answer **B** if the statement in the question is false given the situation described and the facts that are known about it.

Answer **C** if it is impossible to say whether the statement is true or false given the situation described and the facts that are known about it.

Allow yourself 25 minutes.

On the night of 5 November, Abbey Junior School was damaged by fire. The police are treating the fire as suspicious. The following facts are also known:

- Several children were reported to have been letting off fireworks in the school's grounds earlier in the evening.
- There are plans to install security fencing around the school.
- The janitor's storeroom was the only part of the building that was damaged.
- The janitor discovered the fire during a routine inspection and called the fire service.
- The Head Teacher arrived at the school while the fire was being dealt with.
- Nobody was injured.

1 The Head Teacher called the emergency services. ☐

2 The fire was started by fireworks. ☐

3 The janitor had gone specially to the school after hearing about the children playing with fireworks. ☐

4 Several classrooms were badly damaged. ☐

5 There were no casualties. ☐

Agnes Smith, aged 89, was found dead in her bungalow by her 30-year-old grandson. Police are investigating. The following facts are also known:

- Mrs Smith was known to be nervous when she was alone in the house.

- Tom Smith, Mrs Smith's only grandson, was the main beneficiary in her will.

- The house appeared to have been ransacked although there was no sign of a break in.

- Tom Smith visited his grandmother every day.

- Fred Smith, Mrs Smith's son and Tom's father, had argued with his mother the previous day.

- A man had been seen knocking on Mrs Smith's door earlier in the day.

6 Mrs Smith died of natural causes. ☐

7 Fred Smith was not on good terms with his mother. ☐

8 The death was a result of a break-in by an intruder. ☐

9 Mrs Smith was close to her grandson. ☐

10 Mrs Smith knew the intruder who ransacked her house. ☐

Six car stereos were stolen from cars parked in Midchester town centre between 2 pm and 6 pm on the 14 July. It is also known that:

- All the cars were broken into by breaking the front passenger side window.
- The cars all belonged to different people and were parked in different streets and car parks.
- The usual rate of car break-ins in this area is one per week.
- Two young men were seen running across the car park where one theft took place.
- A publican reported that car stereos were being offered for sale by James Croft.
- James Croft has a previous conviction for burglary.

11 The rate of theft from cars is increasing in the area. ☐

12 James Croft stole the stereos. ☐

13 Two men were involved in the thefts. ☐

14 It is likely that the thefts were carried out by the same person(s). ☐

15 The stolen stereos were being sold in local public houses. ☐

A young woman was found dead in her car in a supermarket car park at 6.30 am on Monday 14 October. The following facts are also known:

- The victim died of carbon monoxide poisoning.
- The victim was identified as 23-year-old Sonia Mellor.
- Ms Mellor's mother was called to identify the body.
- The supermarket had been closed since Saturday evening.
- Ms Mellor was known to have extensive credit card debts.
- Ms Mellor lived alone.

16 Ms Mellor may have committed suicide. ☐

17 Both of Ms Mellor's parents are dead. ☐

18 The car containing the body had remained undiscovered for several hours. ☐

19 Ms Mellor lived with her parents. ☐

20 Her extensive debts caused Ms Mellor to commit suicide. ☐

Four cars in Green Street were stolen from their owners' driveways between 11.20 pm and 6 am on Wednesday 14 November. The following facts are also known:

- The stolen cars were all under 2 years old.

- The keys for all the cars had been left near the front doors of the owners' houses.

- One other resident reported hearing suspicious noises at around 1 am.

- A car had been stolen in similar circumstances from a nearby street the previous night.

- There were no house break-ins reported in Green Street.

- Two youths had been reported acting suspiciously and carrying fishing rods in the area the previous night.

21 The two youths stole the cars by fishing for the keys through letterboxes. ☐

22 No cars parked inside garages were stolen. ☐

23 The same method of gaining access to car keys may have been used in all the thefts. ☐

24 All the cars were stolen under cover of darkness. ☐

25 The thief (thieves) stole relatively new cars. ☐

A brick was thrown through the window of a public house at 11.30 pm on Friday 3 March causing damage estimated at £500. The following facts are also known:

- There had been a gang of youths in the public house during the evening who were previously unknown to the landlord.

- Fred Knowles had been barred from the public house for abusive behaviour and left the pub at 9.30 pm.

- Fred Knowles was seen drinking in a public house on the same road between 10 and 11 pm.

- The publican had been unable to obtain insurance cover for window breakages.

- The windows of the public house had been broken several times previously.

- A gang of youths were seen behaving rowdily outside the public house at 11.45 pm.

26 The publican will have to make an insurance claim for the damage. ☐

27 Fred Knowles had a grudge against the publican. ☐

28 The gang of youths broke the window. ☐

29 Fred Knowles was still in the area at 11 pm. ☐

30 This sort of incident is common at this public house. ☐

31 The landlord knew most of the people who were in his pub that night. ☐

TEST 4

(Answers to this test can be found on pages 157–159.)

Here you are given descriptions of situations that a police officer may encounter plus some additional information relating to the incident. Each question is in the form of a statement about the incident and you must decide if it is true using only the evidence you have been given. You should take all the details in the description of the incident, plus the additional information given, to be true. The only decisions you need to make are about the truth – or otherwise – of the numbered statements.

Indicate your answers as follows:

Answer **A** if the statement in the question is true given the situation described and the facts that are known about it.

Answer **B** if the statement in the question is false given the situation described and the facts that are known about it.

Answer **C** if it is impossible to say whether the statement is true or false given the situation described and the facts that are known about it.

Allow yourself 25 minutes.

The Midchester Building Society was held up at gunpoint by two masked men on Tuesday 4 August at 2 pm. They used a white van to make their escape but were apprehended three streets away by the police who also recovered the money. The following facts are also known:

- One shot was fired.
- The customers were made to lie on the floor, while one of the cashiers put the money in a bag.
- A total of five staff were on duty at the time of the burglary.
- The police have arrested and charged two young men.
- No one was injured.
- Police arrived at the building society within 3 minutes of receiving the alarm call.

1 The cashier was shot. ☐

2 The cashier raised the alarm. ☐

3 There was a chase through the streets of Midchester. ☐

4 All the staff and customers were ordered to lie on the floor during the burglary. ☐

5 There were two thieves. ☐

A mother and her two young sons were found dead in their four-bedroom detached home in Barchester-on-Sea on Sunday 4 February. They had all been shot through the head. It is also known that:

- The victims were identified as Jane Smith, aged 35, Tom Smith, aged 9 and Bobby Smith, aged 6.

- Jane's husband, Neil (aged 45) is a senior police officer.

- Neighbours reported that they had heard an argument between Jane and a man on Saturday morning.

- Neil was away for the weekend.

- Jane's mother, Sally, found the bodies when she visited on Sunday afternoon and immediately telephoned the police.

- Neil had been a respected police marksman earlier in his career.

- The house had not been broken into.

6 Sally contacted Neil as soon as she found the bodies. ☐

7 Jane was having an affair. ☐

8 Sally reported the deaths. ☐

9 Neil shot his family. ☐

10 The interior of the house was covered in blood. ☐

Police took a large amount of cannabis and a number of tablets from a house in Barnham at the weekend. The occupier of the house, Paul Bentley, aged 24, was arrested and is being questioned at the local police station. It is also known that:

- Several electrical items were also removed by the police.
- Paul Bentley has a previous conviction for possession of cannabis resin.
- Paul Bentley insisted that the drugs were for his personal use.
- Paul Bentley lives alone.
- Paul Bentley also has previous convictions for criminal damage and burglary.

11 Paul Bentley has been charged with drug dealing. ☐

12 The drugs were for Paul Bentley's personal use. ☐

13 Paul Bentley might be a drugs dealer. ☐

14 Paul Bentley stole the electrical goods. ☐

15 Paul Bentley is a drugs user. ☐

A bus shelter on Walker Street was extensively damaged between 8 pm and midnight on Monday 6 June. It is also known that:

- A lady who lived opposite the shelter called the police at 11.30 pm.

- When the police arrived, there was no one near the bus stop.

- The glass was replaced the following day.

- The glass in this shelter had been smashed on three previous occasions.

- The following day, police questioned two youths about the incident.

16 The lady who reported the incident was able to identify the youths. ☐

17 The police did not catch anyone at the scene on this occasion. ☐

18 Vandalism is a problem in this area. ☐

19 The bus company will not keep repairing the shelters after vandalism of this nature. ☐

20 The police were aware of the identity of the youths who caused the damage. ☐

A car crashed into a tree on Midchester Road at 3.30 pm on Monday 4 May, killing the driver. It is also known that:

- The speed limit on this stretch of road was 50 mph.

- There were no other occupants of the car.

- The driver, Mary Bourne, had a high level of alcohol in her bloodstream.

- Mary usually collected her daughter from school between 3.15 and 3.30 pm each day.

- There were several witnesses to the crash.

- Mary Bourne's speed at the time of the crash was 60 mph.

21 Mary Bourne was driving under the influence of alcohol. ☐

22 Mary had collected her daughter from school as usual. ☐

23 Mary was driving too fast. ☐

24 The witnesses were all drivers. ☐

25 Mary's daughter was left an orphan by the crash. ☐

Twenty-nine people were arrested during a public demonstration to protest against the use of animals in experiments. It is also known that:

- Seven police officers were injured.

- Seventeen protesters were injured.

- The main organisers of the demonstration were the League Against the Use of Animals in Experiments.

- Several shop windows were broken.

- Approximately £16,000 of damage to property was reported.

- The people arrested were charged with public order offences.

26 The protesters were injured by the police while they were trying to maintain order. ☐

27 The only damage caused was to commercial premises. ☐

28 All the protesters were members of the League Against the Use of Animals in Experiments. ☐

29 The police officers were assaulted by the protesters. ☐

30 Twenty-nine people were charged with public order offences. ☐

31 Twenty-four people were injured. ☐

COMPETENCY-BASED STRUCTURED INTERVIEW

This test is designed to test five of the seven core competency areas:

- Respect for race and diversity

- Teamworking

- Effective communication

- Personal responsibility

- Resilience

It takes the form of a structured interview, lasting up to 20 minutes, where you will be asked four questions about how you have dealt with specific situations in the past. The questions are designed to test your abilities in the areas shown above so you must bear this in mind when formulating your answers. It will be beneficial to try to get your ideas together on some of the typical situations you will be asked about – use the following to develop your thoughts in advance. As the interviewer asks you each question, you will be given a written copy of the question to which you can refer. Here are some questions to practise on:

Allow yourself 5 minutes to answer each one.

(Answers to these tests can be found on pages 160–166.)

TEST 1

Tell me something about when you were part of a team.

TEST 2

Describe to me how you responded when you were in a difficult situation.

TEST 3

Could you give me an example of when you have taken other people's views into account?

TEST 4

Tell me about a time when you needed to ask for help.

TEST 5

Describe a situation where you have had to act on your own initiative.

TEST 6

Tell me about a difficult decision you have had to make, and about how you reached your decision.

NB: Make sure that when you choose the examples for your responses to the interview questions, you only select those that you will feel comfortable discussing with the interviewer.

WRITTEN EXERCISES

In these exercises you must assume the role of a newly appointed Customer Services Officer in a Retail and Leisure Centre. So that you have a little information about the job you will be 'taking on', approximately 2 weeks before the assessment centre you will receive a 'Welcome Pack' containing all the information you need about the Retail and Leisure Centre and about the duties and responsibilities of the role. This information is used in these written exercises and also in the interactive exercises. You should read and make sure you understand the information in this pack. It is not necessary to try to remember the contents, however, as you will be given a copy of the pack as part of your preparation for these exercises at the assessment centre. It is important to note here that there is no requirement for you to have any knowledge of police work. To be successful you will need initiative, problem-solving capabilities and an ability to deal with a variety of people, rather than specialised knowledge.

The 'Welcome Pack' Includes the following general documents:

- Customer Service Officer's main duties and responsibilities – i.e. dealing with problems, providing information and liaising between the Retail and Leisure Centre's management, staff and customers.

- Centre Information – opening hours, how many retail units there are and so on.

- Operations Department – details about the Customer Services, Housekeeping and Security teams employed in the Retail and Leisure Centre and the support available on-site from the police.

- Equality Policy Statement – this defines the policy relating to gender, marital status, political opinions, race, disability and so on. It also specifies what should be done if unacceptable behaviour in any of these areas takes place, i.e. asking the person to stop, discussing the problem and then making a formal complaint.

- Code of Conduct – this is a whole list of restrictions on general behaviour within the Retail and Leisure Centre and includes acts of vandalism and theft, barring of animals from the Centre, smoking, sitting on fences, misuse of escalators and other dangerous or disorderly behaviour.

These documents are of course important in that you must use them to ensure that you are carrying out your job properly and are staying within its parameters.

There are two written exercises:

1 You have to write a letter in reply to a letter received from a customer of the Retail and Leisure Centre.

2 You have to prepare a written report in response to a request you have received from the Centre Operations Manager.

You will be given 20 minutes to complete each of these exercises.

It is important to note here that it is the content of your two written pieces that will be assessed and not the layout or neatness. However, the standard of spelling, grammar and punctuation will count towards your final score. We will therefore address the issue of spelling, punctuation and grammar – especially the more common errors that people make – in the Explanations chapter of this book.

One piece of advice before you start these practice questions – remember that it is the core competencies that the assessor is looking out for so be aware of what they are and how you might display your aptitudes in the various areas.

(Answers to these tests can be found on pages 167–180.)

TEST 1 LETTER

Prepare a written response to the following letter from a customer:

9 Meadow View
Castletown
Westshire
16 December 2004

Customer Services Department
Westshire Leisure Centre
Westshire

Dear Sirs,

I have just returned from a visit to the leisure centre and would like to report a problem I found. The floor in the ladies' shower area was dirty and extremely slippy. It seemed to have a slimy feel to it and would probably be dangerous. I was unable to report this to staff at the time as there was no one immediately available.

I hope you will be able to do something about this before someone has an accident.

Yours faithfully,

Carole Shipley (Mrs).

TEST 2 REPORT

Prepare a written response to a request from the Centre Operations Manager, Ashley Cheema. He has asked you for a report on the number of complaints of excess litter that have been reported by customers in the Retail and Leisure Centre in the last 6 months. He keeps statistics on these incidents and says that they have risen sharply.

INTERACTIVE EXERCISES

Before we get to the practice questions, it will be useful to explain the way that these exercises work. During these exercises you are required to take on the role of Customer Services Officer in a Retail and Leisure Centre. As we discussed above, you will have received information about the Centre and about your role in the form of a 'Welcome Pack'.

When you start the interactive exercises, you will be shown to a desk area where you will find all the written information for the first exercise and you will be given 5 minutes to prepare. The information available here will include the 'Welcome Pack' that you will already have seen, and more specific information relating to the exercise. This will set the scene for the situation that you have to deal with when you start the activity phase. There will also be paper for you to make notes at this stage.

NB: You will not be assessed during this preparation phase.

After your 5 minutes are up, you will move to another room (taking your preparatory materials with you) and the activity phase will begin. Also in the room will be a role-play actor and an assessor. There may also be an independent assessor in the room (in effect, examining the examiner, but this should not concern you). Using the information you have acquired during the preparation phase, you should take the initiative, asking relevant questions and responding to what the role-play actor says to you. This specially trained role-play actor will have carefully written guidelines to ensure that they give the correct responses to your questions.

(Answers to these tests can be found on pages 181–187.)

TEST 1

Allow yourself 10 minutes for this exercise.

A store manager from the Retail and Leisure Centre comes to you and tells you that she has seen a known shoplifter in her store and that the shoplifter has now moved on to other shops.

Your task is to formulate the questions you would need to ask the manager and the action you should take.

TEST 2

Allow yourself 10 minutes for this exercise.

You have to deal with a customer who feels that he has been racially abused by another customer.

You must formulate the questions to ask the customer and also consider how you might resolve the situation.

TEST 3

Allow yourself 10 minutes for this exercise.

There have been complaints of disorderly behaviour and vandalism in the Retail and Leisure Centre involving several children from a local school. One of the teachers from that school has come into the Centre to discuss the issue with you. Work out your approach to the problem.

TEST 4

Allow yourself 10 minutes for this exercise.

A member of the Housekeeping team has come to you with a complaint about her treatment by another member of staff. She feels that she is being treated unfairly because of her disability. How will you proceed?

MIXED TEST

And finally in this chapter, here's a test designed to check your ability to move from one type of question to another. It combines all the different elements of the variety of tests you will have to sit during the National Selection Process.

(Answers to this test can be found on pages 187–191.)

Allow yourself 28 minutes to complete this test and no more than 18 minutes on questions 1–14.

Grids are provided for you to show your answers to the numerical and verbal reasoning parts of this mixed test. Make sure that you completely fill in the correct area of the grids for each question to indicate your answer correctly.

NUMERICAL REASONING

ANSWER GRID

	A	B	C	D	E
1	☐	☐	☐	☐	☐
2	☐	☐	☐	☐	☐
3	☐	☐	☐	☐	☐
4	☐	☐	☐	☐	☐
5	☐	☐	☐	☐	☐

	A	**B**	**C**	**D**	**E**
6	☐	☐	☐	☐	☐
	A	**B**	**C**	**D**	**E**
7	☐	☐	☐	☐	☐
	A	**B**	**C**	**D**	**E**
8	☐	☐	☐	☐	☐

QUESTIONS

1 If a family drive 150 miles at an average speed of 50 mph, stop for lunch for 45 minutes and refuel en route taking a break of 10 minutes, at what time would they arrive at their destination if they left home at 9.15 am?

a 1.10 am

b 11.15 am

c 1.15 pm

d 1.10 pm

e 12.10 pm

2 If you were overcharged in a supermarket by £7.05 and found that the reason for the overcharge was that you had been charged for five packets of cereal that you had not had, what would the price of one packet be?

a £1.40

b £1.45

c £1.41

d £0.41

e £0.97

3 If, in a working day of 7.5 hours, you spend 50% of your time working on paperwork, one hour sending and reading e-mails and half an hour in a meeting, how much time would you have left for other duties?

a 2 hours

b 2 hours 15 minutes

c 2 hours 30 minutes

d 2 hours 45 minutes

e 3 hours

4 If burglaries in an area have decreased by 12% from a total for the previous year of 200, how many burglaries have there been in the current year?

a 176

b 184

c 224

d 180

e 212

5 Eleven people work in a section. Four earn £27,500 pa, two earn £19,000 each, one earns £22,500 and the others work part time and earn £22,000 between them. What is the average salary for the section?

a £23,500

b £19,500

c £27,500

d £15,000

e £17,500

6 Ten people were fined a total of £510. If three were fined £100 each, what was the average fine of the remainder?

 a £50

 b £30

 c £100

 d £25

 e £32

7 A charity ball was held and 200 guests paid £45 each to attend. After costs of £200 for room hire, £1000 for the band and £2500 for the meal, what was the amount raised for charity?

 a £9000

 b £14,300

 c £5500

 d £5300

 e £5400

8 A family spends £134 per month on their utility bills. How much would they spend over the course of a year?

 a £1250

 b £408

 c £1560

 d £1340

 e £1608

VERBAL LOGICAL REASONING

The next five questions involve a description of a situation that a police officer may encounter plus some additional information relating to the incident. Each question is then in the form of a statement about the incident and you must decide if it is true using only the evidence you have been given. You should take all the details in the description of the incident, plus the additional information given, to be true. The only decisions you need to make are about the truth – or otherwise – of the numbered statements.

Indicate your answers as follows:

Answer **A** if the statement in the question is true given the situation described and the facts that are known about it.

Answer **B** if the statement in the question is false given the situation described and the facts that are known about it.

Answer **C** if it is impossible to say whether the statement is true or false given the situation described and the facts that are known about it.

Be sure to fill in the appropriate square in the answer grid completely to indicate your answer.

ANSWER GRID

	A	B	C
9	☐	☐	☐

	A	B	C
10	☐	☐	☐

	A	B	C
11	☐	☐	☐
12	☐	☐	☐
13	☐	☐	☐

SITUATIONS AND QUESTIONS

Darren Hill, a local man aged 28, was stabbed in the shoulder outside a public house in the town centre of Newtown at approximately 11.30 pm on Thursday 6 May. He had spent the evening in the pub. No witnesses to the incident have come forward. The following facts are also known:

- Recently the police have been having a crackdown on the carrying of knives in this area.
- Mr Hill is very popular in the area.
- Mr Hill was seriously injured.
- When he recovered, Mr Hill reported that his attacker was similar in stature and age to his father.
- The street was well lit and the weather was fine and clear.

9 Darren Hill was drunk at the time of the attack.

10 A stranger was responsible for the attack.

11 Knife crime is a problem in the area.

12 All the witnesses were too frightened to give evidence.

13 Darren Hill was older than his attacker.

INTERVIEW EXERCISE

Now we come to the interview part of the test. This is competency-based and is designed to test five of the seven core competency areas. These are respect for race and diversity, teamworking, personal responsibility, resilience and effective communication. You must bear these areas in mind when you are formulating your answer to the question below, which will give you valuable practice in this type of situation.

14 Explain what you understand by the term 'respect for diversity' and give an example of when you have encountered this.

WRITTEN EXERCISE

The next question in this mixed test is a written exercise. Make sure you do not spend more than 5 minutes on this part of the test.

15 Write a short letter in reply to the following letter that has been received by Customer Services Department. NB: The details requested are printed in a leaflet that can be sent to the customer.

The Windings
Midchester Road
Maidenhills
29th November 2007

Dear Sir,

Could you please tell me what Aquarobics Classes are available at the Leisure Centre including the days and times they are held, plus the costs.

Thanking you,

Clare Kingsley

INTERACTIVE EXERCISE

The next – and last – question in this mixed test is here to give you practice for the interactive exercises in which you will have to take part during the selection process. Allow yourself 5 minutes for this question.

16 As the Leisure Centre Manager, you are required to hold regular team briefings so that all members of your staff are aware of what is going on at the centre. In this question your task is to prepare for part of one of these meetings by working out your approach to the main problem you have to deal with – vandalism at the centre – and what you will have to tell your staff about it.

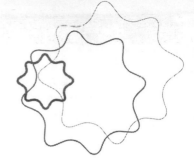

CHAPTER 3
ANSWERS TO AND EXPLANATIONS OF TIMED TESTS

Note the correct answers in each type of test and, even if you have got that one right, read the accompanying explanation. This is where the common pitfalls will be demonstrated and tips given on how to avoid them.

If, after completing these tests, you feel you need further help with numerical reasoning, see *Succeed at Psychometric Testing: Practice Tests for Numerical Reasoning Intermediate Level* and *Succeed at Psychometric Testing: Practice Tests for Numerical Reasoning Advanced Level* in this series.

NUMERICAL REASONING TEST
TEST 1

1 The answer is **b** £1344. Multiply £112 by 12. This might be easier if you split it into two parts, 100×12, and 12×12, then add the two elements together.

2 The answer is **e** 270 miles. The calculation is $9 \times 5 \times 6 = 270$.

3 The answer is **c** £0.85. There are two elements to this multiplication: $(30 \times 1) + (5 \times (12 - 1))$.

4 The answer is **a** 2 hours 20 minutes. Add 1 hour 35 minutes to 45 minutes, remembering it's in hours and minutes.

5 The answer is **b** £43.20. 10% of £48 is £4.80 (£48 ÷ 100 × 10) so take this away from £48.

6 The answer is **d** 29. Subtract 18 from 47.

7 The answer is **a** £175.50. Add the three amounts together, taking care to include the pence in your answer.

8 The answer is **b** 32. Divide by 3 to find a third.

9 The answer is **d** 165 kg. The calculation is (6 × 12) + 93 = 165.

10 The answer is **d** 70 kg. Here you've got six people. Add their weights together and divide by the number of people to find the average weight.

11 The answer is **c** 25 mph. A simple subtraction here.

12 The answer is **a** £93. To solve this multiplication problem you may find it easier to multiply by 2 then by 3 instead of multiplying by 6.

13 The answer is **c** 37 hours. The calculation is (8 × 4) + 5 = 37.

14 The answer is **e** 5. Work out how many boxes it will take (180 ÷ 12 = 15) then subtract from the number of boxes bought.

15 The answer is **b** 200. Simply divide 50,000 by 250 to get your answer.

16 The answer is **d** 252. Three times more vehicles went past than were stopped so this is a simple multiplication.

17 The answer is **b** £24.08. Divide the bill by 3 to get the monthly average.

18 The answer is **c** $\frac{1}{2}$. Add the pies as they are handed out: $1 + \frac{3}{4} + \frac{3}{4} = 2\frac{1}{2}$ so there will be $\frac{1}{2}$ a pie left.

19 The answer is **e** 10%. You are being asked to say what percentage of chairs is not used, i.e. 20 as a percentage of 200 ($100 \div 200 \times 20$).

20 The answer is **a** £57. The calculation is $(4 \times 10) + 20 - 3 = 57$.

21 The answer is **e** 2500. The number of sheets is easy to find – you have 10 reams of 250 sheets each.

22 The answer is **b** 23. The easiest way to do this is to firstly calculate the number of minutes (736) then divide by the number of minutes for one play (32).

23 The answer is **c** £3.60. First find the cost of the amount of electricity used in an hour then multiply by 3 to get your answer.

24 The answer is **e** £84. The part of the question that might catch you out is that the taxi journey is shared so you do not include it twice. The calculation is therefore $(22 \times 2) + (8 \times 2) + 24 = 84$.

25 The answer is **d** 3.5 m. This is a simple question – the carpet is the correct width for one of the room measurements, so the length required will be the other measurement.

TEST 2

1 The answer is **b** 1 kg 250 gms. Here you're adding fractions and numbers – it doesn't matter that they are grams and kilograms.

2 The answer is **e** £262.50. Working out 5% can be easier if you find 10% then halve it. Don't forget to add it back on to the original salary.

3 The answer is **c** £132. Another percentage but this time you must deduct it. To work out 12%, divide £150 by 100 by moving the decimal point two places to the left to find 1% (£1.50) then multiply this by 12 (£18). Then subtract the 12% from the original figure of £150.

4 The answer is **a** 105 hours. Work out each worker's working day (8 hours less 1 hour for lunch) then multiply by 5 then by 3.

5 The answer is **d** £54. Try working out 1% for this one (£10.80) then multiply by 5.

6 The answer is **b** 85. If you divide the number of workers by 6 to get one sixth, then subtract this from the total you will have five sixths.

7 The answer is **e** £53.89. Multiply £4.99 by 12 (it might be simpler to round up to £5 but don't forget to subtract the 12p before you continue) then deduct 10%.

8 The answer is **a** £49.80. Simply multiply 83p by 60.

9 The answer is **c** 384. The calculation is 3 × 4 × 32 = 384.

10 The answer is **d** £215.50. Simply add the three amounts together.

11 The answer is **d** £97.37. Deduct £14.63 from the original amount of £112.

12 The answer is **e** 3430. Simply multiply 490 by 7.

13 The answer is **e** 96. The calculation is
$144 - (144 \div 3) = 96$.

14 The answer is **a** 5 hours 15 minutes. This is easy so long as you remember to use the 24-hour clock, i.e. 14.45 hrs − 09.30.

15 The answer is **e** 0.6 m. The calculation is
$6 - (4 \times 1.35) = 0.6$.

16 The answer is **a** 112. Multiply 4 by 4 then by 7.

17 The answer is **c** 40 minutes. If you travel 30 miles in an hour but only have 20 miles to go, then you will only take two thirds of an hour.

18 The answer is **b** 321. Simply divide 3852 by 12.

19 The answer is **e** 8.25 litres. This is a simple multiplication by 3 using decimals.

20 The answer is **a** 27. The calculation is $81 \div 3$ as you are trying to find one third of the items.

21 The answer is **e** 8. Divide the number of items in total by the number of items per van, i.e. $184 \div 23 = 8$.

22 The answer is **d** 3750. Simply divide 5000 by 4 to find a quarter and multiply by 3 to find three quarters.

23 The answer is **b** £177. Add together the three amounts (£120 + £35 + £203) then deduct the total from the original budget for the garden (£535).

24 The answer is **c** 74°F. The easiest way to work this out is to multiply the average temperature by the number of days, then deduct the temperatures given for the other two days, i.e. (68 × 3) − (64 + 66) = 74.

25 The answer is **e** 90%. As you can easily see that the amount of cash not stolen (£80) is 10% of the total, then the amount stolen must be 90%.

TEST 3

1 The answer is **b** £24.95. Rounding up is the easiest way to go about this question. If one box of pens were to cost £5, then 5 × £5 is simple, then subtract the 5p round-up figure. This rules out some of the suggested answers straight away and, with care, you will quickly get the right answer.

2 The answer is **e** £156.92. The safest route to the correct answer is by jotting down and adding up all the amounts in the question.

3 The answer is **a** £200,000. This is a simple calculation involving an average, i.e. finding the total by multiplying the number of people involved (8) by the average for the group (£25,000).

4 The answer is **a** £75. Simply divide the total money allocated to the overtime by the number of people to arrive at the share for one person.

5 The answer is **e** 67.5 hours. Multiply the number of people by the amount of overtime: 15×4.5.

6 The answer is **d** 56. All you have to do here is divide the total number of people who applied by 4, i.e. $224 \div 4 = 56$.

7 The answer is **a** 176. To find 20% of the figure you have to divide by 5, i.e. $880 \div 5 = 176$.

8 The answer is **a** £231. The first part of your calculation should be £220 $\div$ 100 $\times$ 5 (or £2.20 – if you move the decimal point two places to the left – $\times$ 5) = £11.00, then £220 + £11.00 = £231.00. Don't forget, having found the 5%, to add it back on to the original figure to get the new figure including the 5% increase.

9 The answer is **b** 10%. Here, by restating nine out of ten as $^9/_{10}$, you can see quite clearly the link between fractions and percentages. $^9/_{10}$ is 90% so the remainder is $^1/_{10}$ or 10%.

10 The answer is **c** 80. Despite there being 100 involved in this question, you are not required to work with percentages! This is a simple fraction so divide the number of workers by 5 to get the number who have received training, but remember that you are asked to find the number who have not been trained, so subtract your answer from the original number to get your answer.

11 The answer is **e** 52. Here you are looking for one quarter of 208 so simply divide by 4.

12 The answer is **b** £20.50. Don't waste time here. If you understand that the average is the same as equal shares, then you will not need to work out the total bill and divide by the number of people to get the amount that represents an equal share – you have already been told the answer!

13 The answer is **b** £74.25. Work out 10% of the bill (by moving the decimal point to the left) and then do not forget to add it to the bill to find out the total amount to pay including the 10% tip.

14 The answer is **a** 1 hour 35 minutes. Here you need to find the number of pages to be printed, then divide by the number of pages per minute. Finally convert this to hours and minutes, i.e. $10 \times 76 \div 8 = 95$ minutes = 1 hour 35 minutes. Several of the answers are given in just minutes – do not be fooled into using one of these. The question asks for an answer given in hours and minutes so make sure you ignore any answer that does not comply with this instruction.

15 The answer is **c** £0.391. This is a division problem, i.e. £3519 ÷ 9000 = £0.391. The only aspect that needs extra care is that you get the decimal point in the correct place and you will see that several of the answers are similar except for the decimal point (£3.91, £0.39 and the correct answer £0.391).

16 The answer is **c** 6 hours. One worker would take four times as long to do the job as four workers so multiply $1\frac{1}{2}$ by 4 to get the correct answer of 6 hours.

17 The answer is **a** £94.50. A quick way to work this out is to see that 10% is £9 and half of that would be the 5% that you are looking for, i.e. £4.50 – and don't forget to add the £90 to get your answer.

18 The answer is **d** 70. Here you just need to divide 210 by 3 to find a third.

19 The answer is **e** £300,000. The calculation here is $\frac{1}{2} + \frac{1}{3} = \frac{3}{6} + \frac{2}{6} = \frac{5}{6}$; $\frac{5}{6}$ of £360,000 is £300,000. You could also find a half, then a third and add the amounts together.

20 The answer is **b** 40%. In this question you need to be careful in organising the relevant information you have been given. 1 in 10 = 10%, add this to the 50% and you have the total percentage who are outside the time span given, so the remainder (100 − 60 = 40%) must be what the question requires.

21 The answer is **a** £22. This could be easier if you first find 10% (£2.50) then the other 2% will be a fifth of that (£0.50) so 12% is £3. Then you can deduct that from the original price to get your answer.

22 The answer is **e** 45 hours. At 9 hours per day, 5 days work would be 45 hours.

23 The answer is **b** 8. As 28 days is just 4 weeks, then the answer is $2 \times 4 = 8$.

24 The answer is **d** £373.50. Simply multiply the amount by 3 to get the take home pay.

25 The answer is **a** £13,775. An easy way to tackle this is to work out 10% (£1450), halve it to get 5% (£725) then deduct this from the original price.

TEST 4

1 The answer is **b** £25.50. Simply divide the total by the number of people to find what each friend would have to pay.

2 The answer is **a** £19.25. First find 10% of the fare (£17.50 ÷ 10 = £1.75) then add this back on to the original amount.

3 The answer is **c** 1 hour 20 minutes. First work out the time the printer takes in minutes (10 × 64 ÷ 8 = 80 minutes). You then need to convert this to hours and minutes to comply with the instructions in the question.

4 The answer is **d** £0.22. The easiest way to divide the cost by 5000 is first to divide by 1000 by moving the decimal point three places to the left, then divide your answer by 5. The choices given are confusing so be especially careful with the decimal point.

5 The answer is **a** £1700. To calculate a discount you need to work out the percentage then deduct from the original amount. The calculation is (200 × £10) − (£2000 ÷ 100 × 15) = £2000 − £300 = £1700.

6 The answer is **c** 12 hours. One worker would take six times as long as six workers to complete the same work so you simply need to multiply 2 hours by 6 to get your answer.

7 The answer is **d** 218. This is a simple subtraction
($227 - 9 = 218$).

8 The answer is **e** £63. One way of calculating 5% is by first
finding 10% (which most people find easier) then
dividing your answer by 2. Don't forget to add on the 5%
to show the price after the increase.

9 The answer is **a** 30. This is a straightforward division. To
get a third of something, you divide by 3.

10 The answer is **b** 100. First work out how many people DID
respond to the survey, i.e. 60% + 15% = 75%. This means
that 25% DID NOT respond to the survey and 25% of 400
is 100 (400 ÷ 100 × 25).

11 The answer is **c** 63. Here you simply need to calculate
50% of 126.

12 The answer is **b** 1000. It helps in this question if you
immediately realise that 20% have to be rejected and that
this is the same as one fifth. One fifth of 5000 is 1000.

13 The answer is **d** 82. Just divide the number of workers by
3 to get one third.

14 The answer is **a** 9 minutes. The number of pages being
printed is irrelevant as we know the printing time (10
minutes) and can easily reduce that by 10% to get 9
minutes.

15 The answer is **c** £270. At the normal price two desks
would cost £300. With a 10% discount working out at £30,
this leaves £270 for the new price.

16 The answer is **e** £700. It helps to know that 12½% is the same as one eighth – then you could just deduct the £100 reduction from the original amount. Otherwise you would have to work out 12½% by dividing 800 by 100 then multiplying by 12½.

17 The answer is **b** 385. You just have to work out one quarter of the total workforce here by dividing by 4.

18 The answer is **b** One third. There are three lots of 8 hours in 24 hours so the answer here must be a third.

19 The answer is **c** 60 kg. Work out the weight of each box, then multiply by 3, i.e. 240 ÷ 12 = 20, 20 × 3 = 60.

20 The answer is **b** £6. Divide the total amount (£180) by the number of contributors (30) to find the average.

21 The answer is **d** £1140. Here you simply need to multiply the monthly bill by the number of months, i.e. 95 × 12 = £1140.

22 The answer is **e** £123. Add the three separate amounts together to get the total journey cost.

23 The answer is **a** £52,500. The easiest way to tackle this question is to ignore the zeros initially, then subtract the cost of the goods and the delivery charges from the sales amount.

24 The answer is **c** 105 kg. Simply add 8 kg to the son's weight of 97 kg to get the right answer.

25 The answer is **b** 7½ hours. As the question only asks you how long the woman actually worked, you can ignore the break and the travelling time and just add together the two work periods (3½ + 4 hours).

TEST 5

1 The answer is **c** 6 years. This is an easy one to start this test – 40% is the same as $^4/_{10}$ and the remainder is $^6/_{10}$.

2 The answer is **a** ¼. If you don't read the question carefully you may choose the wrong answer – it asks for a fraction, so don't be fooled into choosing the equivalent 25%.

3 The answer is **e** 11.14. This is a simple matter of adding the total time of 2 hours 40 minutes on to the starting time of 8.34.

4 The answer is **b** 170. 15% of 100 is 15 so 15% of 200 must be 30. You then need to deduct this from the original number of offences.

5 The answer is **b** 35%. With practice, you should immediately be able to see that 20 is a fifth of 100 so you can quickly multiply 7 by 5 to get your answer.

6 The answer is **d** £54. Work this out by multiplying 3 (men) × 2 (hours) × 9 (£).

7 The answer is **e** 2 hours 35 minutes. This is straightforward but you must, of course, remember that there are 60 minutes in an hour so you cannot do a simple subtraction.

8 The answer is **c** £3.94. Simply add the three amounts together.

9 The answer is **c** £350.75. Calculate 15% by dividing £305 by 100 and multiplying by 15, then don't forget to add this back on to the original amount to find the increased figure.

10 The answer is **a** $\frac{1}{8}$. Two of the answer choices here are percentages so you can ignore those. To work out the fraction, divide 200 by 25.

11 The answer is **d** $\frac{3}{4}$. Again, ignore the percentages – you're looking for a fraction as your answer. You should know that 25% is the same as $\frac{1}{4}$ so the remainder must be $\frac{3}{4}$.

12 The answer is **c** 7 PCs, 6 printers. Here you need to work out 50% of the two different items separately then look carefully for the answer among the choices – some of them are deliberately confusing.

13 The answer is **a** £28.53. This is a simple subtraction. £353.53 − £325.

14 The answer is **d** 10 miles. Here you must multiply 4 by 2.5.

15 The answer is **a** £157.80. Add all the amounts together, not forgetting that you must first multiply the ticket price by 2.

16 The answer is **e** 2 kg. Quickly work out the weight of each bag then subtract one from the other to get your answer.

17 The answer is **b** 66. At one pair every 4 months, she will need three pairs per year – then multiply by the number of years given.

18 The answer is **c** 375 m. Multiply 15 by 25 to get your answer.

19 The answer is **d** £114. Work out the cost before discount first then deduct 5% of that total.

20 The answer is **b** $^5/_{12}$. First calculate the number of hours that the lights are on – 14 – then deduct that from 24 and express your answer as a fraction of 24 ($^{10}/_{24}$) and cancel it down to give a proper fraction.

21 The answer is **e** 120. The question is telling you that 5% of the total is 6 so 100% must be 20 times that number.

22 The answer is **e** 12. As you want to get the job done four times faster, you will need four times as many officers.

23 The answer is **b** £4.05. You need to work out only the cost of the top-up of the tank – not the cost of an entire tank of fuel (5 × £0.81).

24 The answer is **a** 12 m. To calculate an average you must add all the values together then divide by the number of values that you have.

25 The answer is **b** 48. Here you are being asked to calculate 75% (or $^3/_4$) of 64.

TEST 6

1 The answer is **a** £7.24. A simple subtraction (£20 − £12.76).

2 The answer is **d** 25%. Here you are being asked to express 2 as a percentage of 8.

3 The answer is **c** 68 kg. Multiply the weight of two chairs (17) by 4 – do not fall into the trap of multiplying by 8.

4 The answer is **b** ⅓ Here you must give 7 as a fraction of 21.

5 The answer is **e** 45 mph. To find the average speed, divide the distance travelled by the number of hours (180 ÷ 4).

6 The answer is **d** 1016. This tests your ability to multiply and to add, i.e. $(192 \times 4) + (2 \times 124) = 768 + 248 = 1016$.

7 The answer is **a** 11 hours 55 minutes. This may be easier if you deal with the hours and the minutes separately. Hours $= (1 + 1) \times 5 = 10$. Minutes $= (13 + 10) \times 5 = 115 = 1$ hour 55 minutes. Then add the two together.

8 The answer is **b** 126. Divide the takings by the price of a ticket to get the number of tickets sold.

9 The answer is **d** £378. Simply multiply £63 by 6.

10 The answer is **a** 7.30 pm. From start to finish, including lunch is 11 hours. Add this on to the starting time to get 19.30 – but since the answer choices do not use the 24-hour clock you are looking for 7.30 pm.

11 The answer is **b** 1.65 m. Here you have a number of calculations to perform, i.e. $(3 \times 1.59) + (2 \times 1.6) + (2 \times 1.79) =$ total height of the people, then divide by 7 (the number of people in the group) to get the average height.

12 The answer is **c** 12 miles. As 15 minutes is a quarter of an hour, it is easy to see that you should divide the speed per hour by 4 to determine the distance travelled.

13 The answer is **d** £9.99. Divide £79.92 by 8 to get your answer.

14 The answer is **b** 97.5 kg. Here you are being asked the total weight of 15 of the parcels (6.5 kg × 15).

15 The answer is **e** £25,750. Find 1% of £25,000 by moving the decimal point two places to the left, then multiply by 3 before adding the 3% back on to the original salary.

16 The answer is **b** 6. Divide the total amount by the amount of paint per room, i.e. 75 ÷ 12.5 = 6. An easy way would be to say two rooms would take 25 litres and the decorator has three times that amount so 2 × 3 = 6 rooms.

17 The answer is **d** £5.25. As there are five lots of 3 minutes in 15 minutes, you should multiply the cost of the call by 5.

18 The answer is **e** £20. There are two ways to tackle this question. Either find the cost of one bottle by dividing £60 by 12, then multiplying by four or, if you realise that four bottles is a third of the case of 12, then you can simply divide £60 by 3 to get the same answer.

19 The answer is **a** 37 litres. Here you should deduct the amount already in the tank from the tank's capacity (60 − 23).

20 The answer is **b** £2808. Simply multiply the average weekly bill by the number of weeks in a year (£54 × 52).

21 The answer is **d** £11.15. A simple subtraction, i.e. £29.60 − £18.45.

22 The answer is **d** 2 hours 50 minutes. This calculation can be made easier if you keep the answers to the two elements of the question in hours and minutes rather than just minutes.

23 The answer is **c** £117. You may find this easier to work out if you add the ticket price to the booking fee and then round it up to £20 before multiplying by 6 – but don't forget to deduct the 6 × £0.50.

24 The answer is **c** 25½ hours. Work out that the PC works 8½ hours per shift then multiply by 3.

25 The answer is **a** ²⁄₉. Cancel down the fraction of ²⁰⁄₉₀ to the right answer of ²⁄₉.

VERBAL LOGICAL REASONING

TEST 1

1 The answer is **B**. The driver – whoever he was – did not stop.

2 The answer is **C**. There is no real evidence here to link the red car with the accident.

3 The answer is **A**. The car was reported stolen earlier that morning.

4 The answer is **C**. The two children MAY have attended the same school but it is not possible to say for sure from the facts given.

5 The answer is **B**. The children were on their way to school.

6 The answer is **C**. We do not know whether or not any goods have been recovered.

7 The answer is **C**. We are not told whether Mr Cornwell has an insurance policy.

8 The answer is **B**. This is untrue as we are specifically told that only items of less than £5 in value were stolen from the sheds.

9 The answer is **C**. Although the youths were trespassing, there is no evidence that they committed the thefts.

10 The answer is **A**. This is stated in the passage.

11 The answer is **C**. The sacked employees may have had grudges but we do not know for sure.

12 The answer is **C**. Although the unidentified cartons may have caused some concern, the scare was caused by the phone call. Also, are we sure that the store man was responsible for the cartons?

13 The answer is **C**. It is not definite that all the personnel were happy to go home.

14 The answer is **A**. As no bomb was found, the call must have been a hoax.

15 The answer is **B**. There was no bomb.

16 The answer is **C**. There is insufficient evidence to prove suicide.

17 The answer is **B**. The victim of the fire was middle aged, whereas the drug addict was only 18 years old, Also, we are not told whether the drug addict was male or female.

18 The answer is **C.** There is no evidence to suggest that the children committed any wrongdoing.

19 The answer is **A.** The post mortem showed that the effects of the fire – smoke inhalation – caused the victim's death.

20 The answer is **C.** We are only informed of one drug addict in the area.

21 The answer is **B.** We know that the woman had two daughters as her elder daughter raised the alarm. She may also, of course, have had sons of which we are unaware.

22 The answer is **A.** If the baby girl was 6 weeks old in early September, then she must have been born in late July.

23 The answer is **C.** This is an assumption and will be one of the things considered during the police investigation.

24 The answer is **C.** It could be true that the neighbour had called the NSPCC but we do not know for sure.

25 The answer is **C.** The mother will be under suspicion but we are not given any information that proves her guilt.

26 The answer is **C.** We are not informed of the gender of the thieves. NB: Not all tax inspectors are men!

27 The answer is **B.** One of the shopkeepers – the owner of the fish and chip shop – was male.

28 The answer is **C.** We do not know if the 'suspicious characters' reported by two shopkeepers were posing as tax inspectors so do not know of any attempts by the 'tax inspectors' that were unsuccessful.

29 The answer is **A**. The team targeted Barchester – a village – and one street in particular.

30 The answer is **C**. It is possible that the owner of the fish and chip shop was trying to avoid paying tax but we are not informed of his motives for falsifying his records. Also, we do not have any information on the tax situation of other shopkeepers.

31 The answer is **C**. As we do not know if any or all of the shopkeepers had insurance cover, we cannot know if they will make claims.

TEST 2

1 The answer is **B**. Paul had previously been cautioned for shoplifting.

2 The answer is **A**. Paul lied about being in school on Tuesday.

3 The answer is **C**. Although it is probable that they have not communicated about Paul's attempt at driving and they are divorced, we do not know any more about their relationship.

4 The answer is **B**. Paul has driven his father's car.

5 The answer is **C**. We are certain about only the two incidences of truancy.

6 The answer is **A**. Molly should not have been allowed to leave with an unidentified person.

7 The answer is **B**. We are told that Molly was kidnapped and it is clear that the person who collected her was not her mother.

8 The answer is **C**. Molly and her sister are usually collected by their mother.

9 The answer is **C**. We know nothing about the girls' relationship.

10 The answer is **C**. We know that the school has a policy that children are not allowed to leave without a parent but we are not told who is responsible for this.

11 The answer is **C**. The bikes have gone, the boys have gone, but we do not know if the boys left of their own free will.

12 The answer is **C**. This may be true but we do not know if they have run away.

13 The answer is **C**. We know that Terry has been bullied at school but we do not know by whom.

14 The answer is **A**. The boys are described in the passage as 'neighbours'.

15 The answer is **B**. The boys were reported missing by their mothers so we know that neither of them is an orphan.

16 The answer is **A**. As the car was new, Carl was unfamiliar with it.

17 The answer is **A**. The other driver is referred to as 'she' in the notes.

18 The answer is **C**. Carl might be a hospital porter, or a nurse, or a radiologist, etc.

19 The answer is **B**. The reason for the other driver not being taken to hospital was because she refused, rather than the extent of her injuries.

20 The answer is **C**. The cause of the collision is not known.

21 The answer is **B**. Theft is the motive.

22 The answer is **A**. He attacked them as they got out of their car.

23 The answer is **C**. Although James Barnes appears to have been waiting for the couple, it may have just been an opportunistic crime.

24 The answer is **B**. The visit of the bailiff would signify money problems.

25 The answer is **C**. This is likely – but we do not know.

26 The answer is **C**. We do not even know if there has been a gas leak.

27 The answer is **C**. This is putting together two facts – the terrorist connections of one of the residents and the politician – and speculating about the connection to the incident.

28 The answer is **C**. Although the caretaker was not the man seen hurrying away from the flats (he is too tall), we do not know whether he was in the area.

29 The answer is **B**. Tom Cross, at 6 feet 3 inches tall, could not be the man described as 'a short, elderly man'.

30 The answer is **C**. There may have been explosives found, we are not told.

31 The answer is **C**. We do not know the cause of the explosion so we cannot say who will be held responsible.

TEST 3

1 The answer is **B**. We know that the janitor called the fire service and also that the Head Teacher arrived at the school while the fire was being dealt with.

2 The answer is **C**. We are not told how the fire started so we should not assume that fireworks were the cause.

3 The answer is **B**. We know that the janitor was on a routine visit to the school.

4 The answer is **B**. We are specifically told that only the janitor's room was damaged.

5 The answer is **A**. We know that nobody was injured.

6 The answer is **C**. The cause of Mrs Smith's death has not been ascertained.

7 The answer is **A**. This is true because of the argument they had the previous day.

8 The answer is **C**. Again, we cannot assume this because we have not been told the cause of death. Also, we do not know whether or not there was any intruder.

9 The answer is **A**. Tom Smith visited his grandmother every day.

10 The answer is **C**. We do not know if the house was ransacked by an intruder or, if it was, whether or not Mrs Smith knew the person.

11 The answer is **C.** To state that the rate of thefts is increasing we would need to show a trend – but we only have details for one day.

12 The answer is **C.** We do not have any proof of James Croft's guilt in this case.

13 The answer is **C.** Although two men were seen running in a car park, we have no evidence that they were involved.

14 The answer is **A.** Note the use of the word 'likely' in this question. It is true that it is 'likely' that the same person carried out all the thefts.

15 The answer is **C.** There is no evidence available that shows us that the stereos offered for sale were, in fact, the stolen ones.

16 The answer is **A.** This is a possibility.

17 The answer is **B.** We know this to be untrue because Ms Mellor's mother identified the body.

18 The answer is **C.** There are no clues in the question as to how long the car – or the body – had been in the car park.

19 The answer is **B.** We are specifically told that Ms Mellor lived alone.

20 The answer is **C.** Although this is a possibility, we cannot know this for sure, given the information.

21 The answer is **C.** This is a possibility – perhaps even a probability – but we do not know for sure.

22 The answer is **A**. We are told that all the stolen cars were taken from driveways.

23 The answer is **A**. It is true that the same method 'may' have been used.

24 The answer is **A**. Between 11.30 pm and 6 am in November it would certainly be dark.

25 The answer is **A**. We are told that all the stolen cars were less than 2 years old.

26 The answer is **B**. The publican does not have insurance cover for window breakages.

27 The answer is **C**. We are not told how Fred Knowles feels about the publican.

28 The answer is **C**. Although they were still in the area and behaving rowdily, we have no evidence that the gang caused any damage.

29 The answer is **A**. We are told that Fred Knowles was drinking in a nearby public house at 11 pm.

30 The answer is **A**. This public house's windows have been damaged several times.

31 The answer is **C**. The landlord MAY have known most of the people in his pub. Alternatively, there may have been an unusual number of strangers in there – we do not know.

TEST 4

1 The answer is **B.** This is untrue as, although one shot was fired, we are informed that no one was injured.

2 The answer is **C.** We are not told who raised the alarm.

3 The answer is **C.** There may have been a chase but we are not told how long it took the police to apprehend the robbers, nor if they followed them from the bank.

4 The answer is **B.** We know this to be untrue because the cashier was putting the money in the bag while the customers were lying on the floor.

5 The answer is **A.** We are told that there were two masked men and that the police have charged two young men.

6 The answer is **B.** The first call Sally made was to the emergency services. We do not know who, if anyone, informed Neil.

7 The answer is **C.** This is a possibility but there is no proof at the moment.

8 The answer is **A.** This is true as Sally rang the police straight away.

9 The answer is **C.** From the information given we do not know who fired the shots.

10 The answer is **C.** This is, at the moment, just in the imagination.

11 The answer is **B.** Paul may be under suspicion of drug dealing but he has not yet been charged.

12 The answer is **C**. Although it is unlikely that the large amount of drugs found was for personal use, we do not know this.

13 The answer is **A**. This is a possibility that the police will be investigating.

14 The answer is **C**. We do not even know that the goods were stolen.

15 The answer is **C**. With a previous drugs conviction and having been found in possession again, Paul is probably a drugs user but we cannot be sure.

16 The answer is **C**. There is nothing to suggest that the lady had been able to describe or identify the youths in question.

17 The answer is **A**. There was no one around when they arrived at the bus shelter.

18 The answer is **A**. The frequency of this type of damage shows that vandalism is indeed a problem.

19 The answer is **C**. Although the bus company has repaired the shelter on this occasion, it may be the last time it does so.

20 The answer is **C**. Although the police questioned two youths, it may be to check what they saw rather than because they are under any suspicion.

21 The answer is **A**. The level of alcohol in her bloodstream has been tested.

22 The answer is **B**. Although she usually collected her daughter, we know that she did not do so on this occasion as there were no other occupants in the car.

23 The answer is **A**. Mary was exceeding the speed limit.

24 The answer is **C**. We do not have any details about the witnesses – they may have been passers-by.

25 The answer is **C**. As we are not given any information about the child's father, we do not know if she is now an orphan.

26 The answer is **C**. We do not know how the protesters were injured.

27 The answer is **C**. We know that some of the damage was to commercial premises but do not know for sure if there was any damage to private premises.

28 The answer is **B**. We know that this organisation is the main organiser of the demonstration – but not the only one involved. Plus, protesters could be supporters of the organisation but not be members.

29 The answer is **C**. We have no details about the causes of the injuries to the police officers.

30 The answer is **A**. We know the number of people arrested – 29 – and that they were charged.

31 The answer is **A**. Adding the number of police officers and of protesters injured gives us this total.

COMPETENCY-BASED STRUCTURED INTERVIEW

As this is an interview where you will have to answer questions designed to assess your aptitudes in the core competencies, it is not possible to give definitive answers to the questions – everyone's answers will be different and yours will be based on your own circumstances and aptitudes and the situations that you have experienced. However, it is possible to give a few general guidelines about your preparation and some more specific advice about the example questions we have provided in these tests.

GENERAL GUIDELINES

- Remember that you should only choose situations that you will feel comfortable discussing with the interviewer.

- Keep in mind the core competencies with which this section of the assessment centre is concerned. You will be assessed on your ability in the areas of respect for race and diversity, teamworking, effective communication, personal responsibility and resilience. You must therefore ensure that the situations you choose will demonstrate the appropriate abilities.

- The interviewer will ask you the question then leave you to answer it but will, if necessary, give you one or two prompting questions to make sure that you give a full answer.

- Thinking about your position on the core competencies in advance of the assessment centre will greatly improve your performance in the interview. The sample test questions in this book will help with this.

- Go through the core competencies one by one and consider how the positive aspects of your character and the experiences you have had can be used to illustrate your capabilities in each of these areas. For example, in the case of teamworking, a positive example would show how you have helped and supported people with whom you have worked (or perhaps played a sport) and how you helped to achieve team goals. A negative example – which you would not want to use, of course – might show that you were not a team player and preferred to work to your own agenda.

- Speak as confidently as you can and make sure that you explain yourself as concisely as possible while still making sure that you get your point across.

- Speak clearly using correct English rather than slang because effective communication is one of the core competencies on which you will be assessed in this section of the assessment centre.

- Try to ask a question or two to check that the interviewer has understood your reply.

ANSWERING THE TEST QUESTIONS
TEST 1

'Tell me something about when you were part of a team.'

Obviously, this question is designed to uncover your attitude towards teamworking. You should choose an example of when you were an active member of a team that achieved what it set out to do. This might be in a work situation or when you were taking part in sports or in further education. Your answer must highlight your role in the team and give details and as many examples as possible (given that you only have 5 minutes per question) of how you:

- Gained the trust of your fellow team members
- Understood your own role in the team
- Built relationships
- Worked effectively as part of a team
- Supported others
- Asked for help when needed
- Developed mutual trust and confidence
- Willingly took on unpopular tasks
- Achieved the team's goals

Don't forget that, although this question requires you to concentrate on the core competency of teamworking, you will also be assessed on the other competencies such as communication or respect for race and diversity, so try to include references in your answer to these attributes too.

TEST 2

'Describe to me how you responded when you were in a difficult situation.'

This is a tricky question aimed at uncovering your resilience and personal responsibility. You will therefore need to show that you are capable of taking personal responsibility for the results you achieve and to display motivation, integrity, commitment and perseverance and also that you are able to remain calm in difficult circumstances. Your answer should demonstrate a logical response to the situation in which you found yourself.

Examples of situations that you might use to demonstrate these attributes could include:

- When you found yourself in some sort of danger
- When you had to sort out an argument between two people
- When you were under pressure in a work situation
- When you had to deal with a difficult emotional issue
- When you had to stand by an unpopular decision you had made
- When you had to deal with confrontation
- When you kept your promise under difficult circumstances

Again, don't forget that your standard of communication will also be assessed.

TEST 3

'Could you give me an example of when you have taken other people's views into account?'

This sort of question will be used to find out your views on teamworking and your level of respect for race and diversity.

You will need to develop your description of the example so that you bring out your attributes in these areas. Discuss, for example, how you obtained advice from someone else when you had a problem or how you went with a majority view in a team situation when you had wanted to go in the opposite direction. Use the opportunity to show that you are able to work with others and that you can see things from other people's points of view. In describing the situation, try to show that you are able to understand and be sensitive to people's problems and needs.

You might, for example, discuss a time when you were working in a team and had suggested a solution to a problem to the team but were met by dissension. If you could also mention that some – or all – of the team members were junior to you and that you could have insisted on your solution being followed but didn't because you could see their point of view despite their junior status or lesser experience, then you will greatly help your case in the area of respect for diversity.

As always you should keep the other core competencies in mind and try to work into your answer the things that will demonstrate your best points.

TEST 4

'Tell me about a time when you needed to ask for help.'

It should not be too difficult to think of good examples for this question and you should choose the example that best displays your ability to work as part of a team, to communicate with others, and perhaps bring personal responsibility into your answer. For example, you may choose to relate your experience when you were working in a team and had to ask for help from your fellow team members to get a task finished to a deadline. This will demonstrate that you are not reluctant to ask for help when necessary and are conscientious about meeting deadlines.

Other situations that you could use include asking for help from fellow workers, friends and family or even strangers. Don't forget, if it's relevant, to bring into the discussion what you have learned from the help you were given. You are trying to present yourself as someone who is open to advice, ready to learn, a good communicator and who deals with situations logically and calmly but with determination to succeed.

TEST 5

'Describe a situation where you have had to act on your own initiative.'

The prime area of competence that you need to relate to in answering this question is that of personal responsibility although, as always, you should keep in mind the other core competencies that are relevant for the structured interview.

Try to think of a situation where you played a leading role and where there is plenty of opportunity to display that you had to take responsibility for problems, come up with your own solutions and then take the necessary action to reach a successful conclusion. To come up with a good example, think about situations such as:

- Work situations where you have had to work unsupervised
- Emergencies at home
- When you were asked for help by someone
- When you had a deadline to meet
- When you took on work without being asked
- When you had to persevere to come up with a solution

Obviously, you will try to avoid any negative aspects of such situations and always try to portray yourself in a good light without being arrogant or boastful – although now is not the time to be over-modest! Negative aspects would include giving up too easily, being unwilling to take on responsibility and not putting in sufficient effort to get the job done.

TEST 6

'Tell me about a difficult decision you have had to make and about how you reached your decision.'

Here you will be concentrating on bringing out your aptitudes in the core competencies of resilience and personal responsibility. You might also be able to include some evidence of your ability to work as part of a team and, of course, while answering the question you will be demonstrating your ability to communicate effectively.

Whatever example you choose to discuss, it should demonstrate quite clearly that you are prepared to make difficult decisions and that you have the confidence to see them through. You should make points that show that although you were dealing with difficult circumstances, you remained calm and were still able to think logically and decisively. Make sure that you explain your decision-making process so that it is clear to the interviewer that you did not reach your decision too quickly or without considering the full facts of the situation and that, where appropriate, you took others' views into account.

Everyone's perceptions and examples of difficult decisions will be different but some types of decision you might want to consider include:

- A career change
- A decision to move house
- A decision where you knew there would be opposition
- A decision where there were a lot of different facts to be taken into account

Again, try to avoid negative aspects of your decision-making process. If you leave the interviewer with the impression that you worry unduly about making mistakes and that this might lead to you avoiding difficult decisions, you will not have acquitted yourself well.

WRITTEN EXERCISES

Most people who worry about these written exercises will focus on their lack of ability in spelling, punctuation and grammar – and these are important elements of these exercises so there is plenty of advice on these aspects in a moment – but it is of paramount importance that you keep in mind the main purpose of these exercises. That is for the people conducting the assessment centre to recruit the right candidates, i.e. those who can demonstrate that they possess the abilities and skills encompassed by the core competencies. For this reason you should 'read between the lines' of the written exercises and think carefully about what opportunities are being offered to you to demonstrate your abilities. Ask yourself how you can use this letter or report to display each of the core competencies. (You will find it useful here to refresh your memory about these competencies – turn back to Chapter 1 and read through the details of the seven core competencies.) Clearly, you will not be able to include each of the competencies in every exercise but it should be apparent to you which ones you are being assessed for. This is a fairly straightforward task. Here are a few quick checks you can make as you read the questions and formulate your answers:

- Consider the person who wrote the letter. How would you describe them? Remember 'respect for race and diversity' and 'community and customer focus' here, for example.

- Put yourself in the place of the letter writer – what sort of response are you expecting or hoping for? Concentrate on the 'problem solving' and 'community and customer focus' competencies.

- Think about the action you can take to resolve the problem and tailor your response to fit the person who has written the letter. Again your 'problem-solving' skills will be under scrutiny here and also 'personal responsibility' and, of course, 'effective communication'.

Having decided upon the relevant competencies, you can then make sure that you highlight, by tailoring your answer accordingly, the appropriate skills.

As we have already said, during these tests the content of your written responses will be assessed rather than the layout so, although you should try to keep the look of the letter and the report neat, there is no requirement for you to know the finer points of letter layout and there is no standard, accepted format for the report.

What will be assessed, in addition to your content, is your use of grammar and punctuation and correct spelling. As this is something that worries many adults who may have left school several years previously, we will therefore give you a few pointers to help you along in this area. The most important things to remember are detailed below.

CONTENT

- Answer the question!
- Keep to the point
- Cover the key points
- Keep in mind the person(s) who will be reading your document and tailor your approach accordingly – try to 'put yourself in their shoes'
- Keep it concise
- Be polite
- Show that you have solved the problem, or make suggestions for consideration, taking into account all the information you have

- Structure is important – remember letters and reports should have a beginning, a middle and an end
- Use paragraphs (a separate one for each point that you need to make) and complete sentences
- Always proofread your letter or report

WRITING LETTERS

- Try not to send letters addressed 'Dear Sir or Madam' – always use the name of the recipient whenever possible
- Make sure that your letter is well structured – with a beginning, a middle and an end
- You might find it helpful to add a subject heading as this will immediately announce the purpose of your letter and it can also make it easier to file the letter correctly; put this on the line below 'Dear . . .', before you start your opening paragraph
- Always proofread your letter before you send it
- Do not use slang phrases, abbreviated words or very informal language – remember that this is a business letter written in your capacity as a Customer Services Officer
- One last piece of advice about writing letters – do not start with 'I am writing . . .' – that is just too obvious

WRITING REPORTS

A report is usually written following some sort of investigation or research and contains your conclusion or perhaps your recommendations for action to be taken. If you are asked to report on a subject you should:

- Make sure that you know exactly what is required
- Find sufficient information on the subject to enable you to do justice to the task
- Try to be unbiased – any opinions must be backed up with facts
- Give your report a short, clear title
- Structure is important – remember that reports should have a beginning, a middle and an end
- Start with a summary of why you are preparing the report
- Decide upon a logical order
- Use headings to make the document clearer
- End with your conclusions or recommendations and make sure that these always follow on logically from the information you have presented in your report
- Sign and date the document

SPELLING, GRAMMAR AND PUNCTUATION

Following the rules of spelling, punctuation and grammar in all business communications is extremely important. They make your letters, reports and memos easier to read and understand. If you make mistakes in any of these vital areas, your reader will have to pause to puzzle out what is being said. For instance:

- A comma or full stop in the wrong place will interrupt the flow of your writing
- An incorrect spelling will distract the readers while they work out what the mistake is
- Poor grammar will make it difficult for readers to work out the sense of what you are trying to say

It is not always easy to become perfect in these areas but awareness of the problems plus an extra effort to check your work will help to ensure that you communicate exactly what you mean to say and get a good score in the area of effective communication.

GRAMMAR

Let's look at some of the more common grammatical errors:

VERB AND SUBJECT AGREEMENT

Mistakes in this area sound awful in conversation and may be soon forgotten, but if you make the same mistake in writing, it will be there for all to see and your organisation may be judged by the quality (or lack of quality!) of its materials. If a verb is singular then its subject must be singular too. Or both must be plural. For instance, we say 'He (the subject) is (the verb) handsome' and never 'He are handsome' and 'They were late' rather than 'They was late'. This rule applies even if the subject is a word such as none, neither or either (all of which are singular), or collective nouns such as the committee, the Government or the Board – all of which are also singular. We would therefore say, 'The committee has already given its decision on this' rather than 'The committee have already given their decision on this'.

DOUBLE NEGATIVES

If you use two negative words in a sentence, they will not express what you meant to say as they will cancel each other out. For example, 'I don't know nothing'. This can be corrected by taking out one of the negatives. So either 'I don't know anything' or 'I know nothing' would make sense.

USING 'I' OR 'ME'

The trick to deciding whether to say 'you and I' or 'you and me' is to see if you can substitute 'we' or 'us'. If 'we' makes sense, then use 'you and I'. If the sentence makes sense using 'us', then it would be correct to say 'you and me'. For instance, we would never write 'The Head Teacher invited you and I to the meeting'. Using the rule of 'we or us', it would not make sense to say 'The Head Teacher invited we to the meeting' so 'you and I' is also incorrect. 'The Head Teacher invited you and me to the meeting' is correct.

PAIRS OF WORDS

Some pairs of words frequently cause difficulties. These include:

- Neither/nor and either/or. These pairs should not be spilt up. It is not correct to say, for example, 'Neither the boy or his sister arrived on time'.

- Shall/will and should/would. More pairs of words that belong together. If you use one of them in a sentence then you should use the second one. For example, 'I shall be pleased if you will come with me' or 'I should be pleased if you would come with me'.

- Learned and taught. You can learn a subject or be taught something but the two words are not interchangeable. You should never write 'He learned me how to do it'.

- Lend and borrow. The rule here can be remembered as 'I lend to, you borrow from'. Applying this rule, you can see that it would be incorrect to say 'I borrowed you £5'.

SPLIT INFINITIVES

Infinitives are the basic forms of verbs. For example, to go, to learn, to write. You should not try to put another word in the middle as this will result in a split infinitive. Examples of split infinitives include 'to boldly go' (as famously included in the opening line of *Star Trek!*), 'to quickly learn' and 'to carefully write'. The way to avoid this is to change the order of the words. Say 'to go boldly', 'to learn quickly' and 'to write carefully'.

AMBIGUOUS SENTENCES

If what you write can mean two different things, then you are being ambiguous and that is never good in business dealings. An example of this might be 'I need to leave badly'. This could mean that you need to make a poor exit or, more likely, you really need to leave. Confusion can also be caused by the careless use of pronouns. When you use a pronoun – he, she, they etc. – it should be absolutely clear to whom you are referring. If there is any doubt, it is safer to use the person's full name.

COMPARATIVE WORDS

Deciding which word to use when comparing two or more people or objects is easy if you follow the rules relating to the numbers involved. If you are comparing only two things, words usually have '-er' added to them and if you are comparing more than two, you should add '-est'. So you would write 'The Head Teacher arrived later than the Deputy Head' and 'Of all the staff, the Head Teacher arrived latest'.

You should note that some words are exceptions to this rule, as you cannot put '-er' and '-est' on the end of them. In this case you would put 'more' in front of the word when comparing two objects and add 'most' when comparing more than two. For example, 'She was more beautiful than her sister' and 'She was the most beautiful of all the sisters'.

AT THE END OF A SENTENCE

You should not use a preposition (words such as of, to, for, about) at the end of a sentence. They make your sentence sound clumsy. Examples of this type of error include 'The manager is the one you will be reporting to'. To avoid this you could rephrase the sentence. In this case you might say 'You will be reporting to the Manager'. Often, with this type of error, you will need to use 'whom' instead of 'who'. For instance, 'Who will you be reporting to?' could be replaced with 'To whom will you be reporting?'

PUNCTUATION

Punctuation causes many problems for a lot of people but it is well worth making the effort to get it right as it will make your written communication much easier to understand. In spoken communication we pause naturally to make our meaning clear, and punctuation marks such as full stops, commas and semi-colons are designed to show the reader where the pauses come. Some people use a 'pepper-pot approach' to punctuation – sprinkling commas and full stops throughout their work. This does not help to raise the standard of the work any more than missing out the punctuation altogether, so it is worth learning a few basic rules to ensure that the punctuation you use makes your work easier to understand.

APOSTROPHES

Apostrophes are the most common cause of punctuation problems in this sort of test. There are two uses for an apostrophe:

1 To show possession. For example the apostrophe in the phrase 'the Head Teacher's office' shows that the office belongs to the Head Teacher. It can often be difficult to decide where to put the apostrophe, especially when a plural is involved. To help with this decision you should ask yourself who owns the object. If the answer is singular, then the apostrophe should be placed between the last letter of the singular word and the 's' that shows ownership. If the object is owned by more than one person, then the apostrophe must be placed after the 's' that denotes that it is plural. So, with only one teacher for example, we would write 'the teacher's books' but with several teachers we would write 'the teachers' books'. NB: The exception to this possessive rule is 'its'. When 'its' refers to ownership of something, there is no apostrophe.

2 To show where letters are missing, for example, 'don't' for do not, 'it's' for it is, 'can't' for cannot, 'we're' for we are.

COMMAS, SEMI-COLONS AND FULLSTOPS

Commas, semi-colons and full stops are not interchangeable. They each have their correct place in a sentence and can be used to create pauses of differing lengths.

- Full stops come at the end of sentences and represent the longest pause. It is used to show the end of the thought contained in that sentence. The next sentence will then begin with a capital letter.

- Commas and semi-colons, on the other hand, come in the middle of sentences and denote pauses of shorter length. Semi colons give a shorter pause than a full stop but a longer one than a comma. Commas give a short pause and are most often used to separate items in lists within a sentence.

SPELLING

A lot of people lack confidence in their ability to spell. English spelling is not easy but some people find it more difficult than others and it is not possible just to 'learn a few rules' to solve the problem completely – but it can help. If you feel that you're a competent enough writer to get through the police tests but are worried that your spelling will let you down, this next section is for you.

The reasons why people sometimes get spellings wrong in English – apart from it being a language full of irregularities – are varied and include:

- Spelling it as it is pronounced. This works with some words like 'sat' or 'fin' for example but some words are spelled nothing like how they sound – 'yacht' is not spelled 'yot' for instance.

- Missing a letter out. This is quite often done when a word contains double letters such as 'address' or 'accommodate'.

- Including an extra letter. Again this is most likely to happen when a word contains double letters – or does it?

- Changing letters around. Transposing two letters is a common error – writing 'beleif' rather than 'belief' for example.

- Getting two words mixed up. Examples of words that are often confused include where/were/wear, there/their/they're and your/you're.

Many words just have to be learned, but some difficulties can be overcome by paying attention to some rules such as:

- 'i' before 'e' except after 'c' – when the sound is long ee. This will help you with words such as 'belief' and 'receive'.

- Adding 'ise', 'ize' or 'yse' to the end of words. Many words can be spelled in more than one way but most can be spelled using 'ise'. Some notable exceptions are capsize, analyse and paralyse.

- Use 'c' if it's a noun and 's' if it's a verb. Some words sound the same but are spelled differently according to whether they are nouns or verbs. So, for example, use advise, practise and prophesy if you need a verb (a 'doing' word) but use advice, practice and prophecy when a noun (the name of a thing) would be correct.

Now we get to the words that are awkward to spell but don't follow the rules and so we just have to learn them. If there are words that you know you are doubtful about, get into the habit – even if just for the week or two before your assessment centre – of looking the word up in a dictionary. Otherwise, test yourself on this list of commonly misspelled words:

Accelerate	Accident	Accommodation
Achievement	Acknowledgement	Acquaintance
Adequate	Always	Analysis
Awful	Beautiful	Beginning
Behaviour	Believe	Cemetery
Character	Committed	Compulsory
Condemn	Correspondence	Criticism
Deceit	Definite	Deliberately
Discipline	Embarrass	Excellent
Exaggerate	Exceptional	Expense
Extraordinary	February	Foreign
Guarantee	Harassment	Immediate
Interrupt	Knowledge	Liaise
Manoeuvre	Necessary	Neither
Obedient	Occur	Opinion
Ordinary	Permission	Prevalent
Proceed	Receive	Responsible
Sentence	Separate	Sincerely
Succeed	Sympathy	Tomorrow
Unfortunately	Unnecessary	Yesterday

TEST 1 LETTER

In replying to this specific example of a letter to the Customer Services Officer about the condition of the ladies' shower area in the Retail and Leisure Centre, you will have to be reassuring without being complacent. Address Mrs Shipley by name and lay out your letter in a similar format to her letter. There are a number of issues for you to answer, so tackle them one by one:

- The cleanliness of the ladies' shower area and what will be done to improve the situation
- The health and safety aspect of the problem
- Thanking Mrs Shipley for her concern and her action
- Reassuring Mrs Shipley that the situation will not be allowed to happen again

TEST 2 REPORT

Here you will have to compile a report giving details of the type of complaints received and how you have dealt with them. The Centre Operations Manager will also want to see that you have taken the issue seriously and that you have solid plans for reducing the number of complaints in the future. You will therefore have to detail your improved litter-picking routines, and you may want to consider mentioning a publicity campaign to make people aware of the problem caused by litter. Obviously, you do not have a great deal of time to conjure up these plans, so keep the details brief.

INTERACTIVE EXERCISES

Although it is not possible to replicate the interactive exercises exactly here – role-play actors don't come with the book! – learning about the process and giving yourself some time to consider your approach to the various types of problem you may meet and to formulate the questions needed to extract the relevant information will undoubtedly help your preparation for the assessment centre.

Before we look at the specific situations and your approach to the solutions, there are some general guidelines that will help you in this type of exercise.

GENERAL GUIDELINES

- You must take the initiative in the activity phase – have your questions ready.

- Remember that the role-play actor has to comply with the guidelines he or she has been given and may not give you information unless you specifically request it.

- You must adhere completely to the policies set down in the documents you have been given. So, for example, smoking is only allowed in designated areas. If a customer were found smoking outside those areas, you would have to deal with the problem.

- Try to empathise with the person with whom you are required to interact. Think about what you can do to put them at their ease.

- Remember that you will be assessed during each activity phase and the examiner will be looking for evidence that you have the core competencies.

- The trained assessor will make a written assessment of what you do and how you do it during the activity phase.

- You are not required to have any knowledge of the law or police procedures and previous experience of customer service is not necessary.

- Be polite, firm, but sensitive at all times.

- In formulating your approach to the situation, keep in mind the purpose of the exercises – they are for the assessor to find out whether you meet their criteria in terms of the core competencies.

- Remember that respect for race and diversity is assessed in all the tests and exercises.

ANSWERING THE TEST QUESTIONS

TEST 1

'A store manager from the Retail and Leisure Centre comes to you and tells you that she has seen a known shoplifter in her store and that the shoplifter has now moved on to other shops.

Your task is to formulate the questions you would need to ask the manager and the action you should take.'

Your first step here should be to alert the security department to the problem. Obtain details from the store manager comprising a description of the shoplifter including clothing, the time spotted, and if possible the name of the suspect. You may also need to find out whether CCTV footage could provide possible evidence or assistance to the security team. You should not, however, try to do the security team's job for them. Be brief and pass the information to the right people while reassuring the store manager that every effort will be made to track down the shoplifter.

A number of core competencies will be assessed during this exercise including teamworking, community and customer focus, effective communication and problem solving in addition to the all-important respect for race and diversity. In particular, your ability to solve problems and gather information will be highlighted.

During the preparation phase you should have worked out your questions and what you planned to do, working within the parameters of your role and the information you have been given about the workings of the centre.

TEST 2

'You have to deal with a customer who feels that he has been racially abused by another customer.

You must formulate the questions to ask the customer and also consider how you might resolve the situation.'

Here you will obviously have to be aware of the sensitivities of the customer who feels that he has been abused. Get specific details of the incident about which he is complaining and then follow the procedure as laid down in the Equality Policy, i.e:

1 If the other customer is still around and if the unacceptable behaviour is still going on ask the person to stop. Note that some people may not be aware that their behaviour is causing offence or harm and may stop if asked politely.

2 If you are unsure what to do next – perhaps you don't know for sure whether the incident constituted harassment – seek advice from your manager. Remember that asking for help will not be counted against you during the assessment as the ability to ask for help when needed is an important part of teamworking. Someone who carried blindly on even when they didn't know what they were doing would usually be penalised.

3 Assist the customer in making a formal complaint to the Centre Operations Manager if necessary.

Throughout your dealings with this customer you should try to act in a reassuring and respectful manner. Your ability to keep control of the situation and of yourself will be under scrutiny.

Apart from teamworking and, as always, respect for race and diversity, the core competencies that will be assessed here are community and customer focus and effective communication. You must therefore ensure that you listen carefully to the complaint and adapt your style of communication to meet the needs of the complainant. Make sure that he is kept informed at every stage of what you are doing about his complaint and why. You need to show your understanding and empathy with the customer's complaint – you would not get away with, for instance, acting as if you had never encountered racial prejudice before.

TEST 3

'There have been complaints of disorderly behaviour and vandalism in the Retail and Leisure Centre involving several children from a local school. One of the teachers from that school has come into the Centre to discuss the issue with you. Work out your approach to the problem.'

The main core competency being assessed here will be community and customer focus. You will need to show your understanding of the community – of which the local school is, of course, a part – and of the issues involved. Try to ensure that you see the situation from all points of view. It is possible that the teacher will be defensive of the children's actions. On the other hand, they may be in full agreement with the complaint, so you will have to tailor your approach to meet the circumstances.

In the preparation phase, try to think of possible solutions to what is probably an ongoing problem in the Centre. Be ready to discuss your suggestions with the teacher. Solutions might include:

- Restricting the hours that the children are allowed to come into the Centre, for example, outside school hours or weekends only

- Only allowing the children to come into the Centre if accompanied by an adult

- Only allowing the children to come into the Centre if they have obtained a note from a parent or teacher

Be prepared to discuss the pros and cons of each solution and to listen to any solutions the teacher may suggest.

TEST 4

'A member of the Housekeeping team has come to you with a complaint about her treatment by another member of staff. She feels that she is being treated unfairly because of her disability. How will you proceed?'

Here again your respect for race and diversity and your understanding of the different problems people face will be to the fore. You will need to act with tact and diplomacy and again be patient and tolerant when dealing with both of the parties to this situation. You must make them feel valued by listening carefully and showing that you understand the problem from both points of view.

Obviously, your communication skills play an important part in this situation. You should be careful not to be dismissive or impatient and you must on no account show any bias when dealing with the people involved.

Your first task will be to get the details of the complaint from the member of the Housekeeping team. Try to draw out the exact details of the action(s) that she feels are discriminatory. You may wish to consider the following questions:

- Exactly what happened?
- When?
- Who else was involved? (Did anyone witness the treatment that she believes is unfair?)
- What was said to her?
- How did she react?
- How did it make her feel?

When you've asked a question, be sure to listen to the answer. This is a vital part of effective communication.

When you feel you have got all the information that is forthcoming, you will need to get the views and comments of the person being complained about – remember tact and diplomacy and also, whenever possible, conduct this sort of enquiry face to face rather than over the telephone. It is imperative that you do not make a judgement at this stage. You must first get the different points of view.

Your problem-solving skills will also be assessed during this exercise so you need to show that you are capable of obtaining and assimilating information and then using it effectively to reach a decision on the action to take. Try to demonstrate during the exercise that, if appropriate, you can see what can and can't be changed and can make a good decision that takes into account all the relevant points. Problem solving is a key part of the role that you are being asked to play during these exercises – just as it is also, of course, a vital part of police work – so you need to show this aptitude clearly to the assessor.

Issues of personal responsibility will also be under scrutiny – standing up for what is right might be called for here and you must follow the situation through to its satisfactory conclusion.

MIXED TEXT

1 The answer is **d** 1.10 pm. If you travel at an average speed of 50 mph, it will take you 3 hours to go 150 miles. To this you need to add the break, i.e. 45 minutes + 10 minutes. So your journey takes a total of 3 hours 55 minutes. Try adding 4 hours to your start time then taking off 5 minutes.

2 The answer is **c** £1.41. Here you simply need to divide the overcharge by 5 to get your answer.

3 The answer is **b** 2 hours 15 minutes. First you need to find the time spent on all the tasks mentioned then subtract from the working day, i.e. 7.5 − (3.75 + 1 + 0.5) = 2.25.

4 The answer is **a** 176. As 12% of 200 is 24, this should be subtracted from the 200 to give the current year's number of burglaries.

5 The answer is **e** £17,500. To find an average salary you must find the total amount of salaries then divide by the number of workers. Care should be taken here to note that the part-time workers do not earn £22,000 each, but £22,000 between them. So, the calculation is ((27.5 × 4) (2 × 19) + 22.5 + 22) ÷ 11 = 17.5.

6 The answer is **b** £30. This is a similar question to the previous one. First you must deduct the fines of 3 people then divide by the remainder (not the total number of people) to get their average fine, i.e. 510 − (100 × 3) divided by 7 = 30.

7 The answer is **d** £5300. In this question you should first work out the income for the event then deduct the total of the costs, i.e. (200 × 45) − (200 + 1000 + 2500) = 5300.

8 The answer is **e** £1608. Finding the answer to this question is simply a matter of multiplying 134 by 12.

9 The answer is **C**. Although we know that the victim had been in the pub prior to the attack, we do not know whether or not he was drunk.

10 The answer is **C**. As we do not know the identity of the attacker, it is impossible to say whether he was a stranger to the victim. As far as we know, Darren has not said whether his attacker was known or unknown to him.

11 The answer is **A**. We know this to be true because we have been told that the police are trying to control the carrying of knives in the area.

12 The answer is **C**. We are not given any reasons why no witnesses have come forward. It may be that they are frightened but we cannot say for sure from the information we have been given.

13 The answer is **B**. As Darren specifically says that his attacker was about the same age as his father, it is true to say that the attacker was older than Darren.

14 Your preparation for your test should include a study of the core competencies. Respect for race and diversity is an important one and involves treating everyone you meet with respect and dignity. You should be able to give examples of diversity that you may come across – race, gender, religion, status and so on – and be able to show how you deal with this in your daily life. You might, for example, point to having worked with both men and women, having friends who are gay, or having some knowledge of different religions. A good example to think about in advance might be where someone you know has expressed narrow or prejudiced views about a particular group and how you felt about this.

15 This is a straightforward question that asks you to write a short letter. If you know the basics of standard letter layout then this, although not essential, will help you in the presentation of your answer, so note the simple layout below. You are told that there is a leaflet available containing all the information that Clare Kingsley has requested so this makes your task easy. Here is an example of how you might reply:

Leisure Centre
High Street
Maidenhills
5th December 2007

Ms C Kingsley
The Windings
Midchester Road
Maidenhills

Dear Ms Kingsley,

Thank you for your letter dated 28 November. I have pleasure in enclosing our leaflet 'Classes at Maidenhills Leisure Centre', which I believe contains all the information you have requested.

If there is anything else I can help you with, please do not hesitate to get in touch.

Yours sincerely,

J. Bloggs – Leisure Centre Manager

16 To arrive at an answer to this question, you will have to give some thought to how a Leisure Centre Manager might solve the problem of vandalism. Think about actions he or she may take, who might help, time scales, how the tasks can be delegated and so on.

The Leisure Centre Manager might make notes to use during the meeting as follows:

1 Outline the problem
- costs of vandalism per year approx. £20,000
- problem areas – windows, lockers, gym equipment

2 What can we do?
- vigilance – regular visits (every half hour) to locker and gym areas by nominated staff to check equipment being used correctly and no-one loitering in locker areas
- alert police – Assistant Manager to liaise weekly, Manager to put up posters asking for help from the public

These notes could then be submitted as your answer as they outline your approach to the problem and what you will tell your staff.

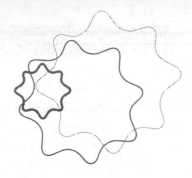

CHAPTER 4
DIAGNOSIS AND FURTHER READING

In this final chapter, we will look at how the exercises that you will be set during the assessment centre are scored.

ASSESSMENT CENTRE SCORING

As we mentioned earlier in the book, the National Selection Process is a series of standardised tests. The first two tests – the numerical reasoning and verbal logical reasoning tests – will be marked, and then your test scores are converted into a grade based on a scale from A to D given for the two combined tests, with As being given to the very highest performing candidates and Ds to the ones who have performed less well.

MARKING SCHEME

To check your progress in either the numerical reasoning or verbal logical reasoning tests featured in this book, go through all of the tests that you have completed. For each test there is a potential 'raw' score as follows:

- Numerical reasoning – 125 marks (5 marks for each of the 25 questions)

- Verbal logical reasoning – 155 (5 marks for each of the 31 questions)

Mark each answer as correct or incorrect. Each question correctly answered scores 5 marks as follows.

Correct answers	1	2	3	4	5	6	7	8	9	10
Score	5	10	15	20	25	30	35	40	45	50

Incorrect answers score zero marks.

For example, a verbal logical reasoning test with 26 questions correct, 3 incorrect, 2 not attempted, would score as follows:

26 correct $\times$ 5 marks = 130
3 incorrect $\times$ 0 marks = 0
2 incomplete $\times$ 0 = 0
Test score = 130

Now use the following charts to interpret your final score for each test:

NUMERICAL REASONING

Well below average	Below average	Average	Above Average	Well above average
0 to 35	40 to 55	60 to 75	80 to 100	105 or over

VERBAL LOGICAL REASONING

Well below average	Below average	Average	Above average	Well above average
0 to 45	50 to 75	80 to 100	105 to 125	130 or over

If your score is 'Above average' or 'Well above average', you may decide that you would like to spend more of your preparation time on other sections of the test. If the results indicate that your score is 'Below average' or 'Well below average', keep practising. As you work through the tests, you should see an improvement in the scores you achieve.

Whatever your score, do not allow yourself to be discouraged – tests are only part of the interview process and it is possible to improve with practice.

In the remaining exercises – the interview, the written exercises and the interactive exercises – your performance in each competency area within an exercise will be assessed and given a grade on a scale from A to D. This is based on what you did in the exercises and how you did it. You will not be assessed on knowledge of specific police procedures. By reading the notes in the Explanations chapter, you should have been able to assess your aptitude in each area. Remember that these exercises are specially designed to assess the core competencies and you will improve your performance if you formulate your answers with these specific aspects in mind.

The assessment process is very carefully worked out so that during the assessment centre each of the seven core competencies will be assessed at least three times in different exercises and by different people.

A grade D in any of the four areas – the reasoning tests, the competency-based structured interview, the written exercises or the interactive exercises – will result in failure of the assessment centre. Whether you have passed or failed, you should receive notification in writing within about 10 days.

SUGGESTIONS FOR FURTHER IMPROVEMENT

PROBLEMS AND PITFALLS

Now that you have worked through the questions, answers and explanations, we can look at the problems and pitfalls associated with tests in general. For example, it is absolutely essential that you read the instructions carefully. Ask yourself a few questions as you read:

- What exactly are you being asked to do?
- How should you indicate your answers?
- Can you write on the question paper?
- Has some spare paper been supplied for the purpose of rough calculations or for jotting down notes?
- Do you need to estimate the answer?

These are general things that you should look out for but there are also some pitfalls that are associated with specific types of questions. You will find many of these highlighted in this book when the individual questions are explained (see Chapter 3). Here are a few guidelines for avoiding some of the problems and pitfalls you may come across:

- With tests where you have to write your answers on a separate sheet of paper, check from time to time that you are writing your answers in the right place. It is easy – especially if you have to miss out a difficult question or are working under time constraints – to continue down the answer sheet totally unaware that your answers are wrong simply because they are written in the wrong space.

- Avoid spending too much time on a difficult question.

- Don't guess. You may need to estimate an answer in the numerical section or make a reasoned selection in the logic test but do not resort to wild guessing.

- In the verbal logical reasoning test, make sure that you do not assume things to be true that, from the information you are given, could probably or possibly be true.

THE VALUE OF PREPARATION

Unfamiliarity gets in the way of your natural ability, so practice is an invaluable form of preparation. An Olympic runner does not just turn up at the track and set off as fast as she can – she will practise extensively, treat her mind and body well and find out all she can about the race. Why should taking any other sort of test be different? So make the most of your period of preparation. Practice is the most important element of your preparation strategy. The timed tests in Chapter 2 will help with that. Aim to practise for up to 2 hours in any one session. Any more than that may be counter-productive. It is almost impossible to sustain the intense concentration needed for any longer than 2 hours.

What other forms of preparation should you consider? Apart from the intensive practice that you can take advantage of by using the timed tests, there are other sorts of practice. For example, to help with the numerical test you should make yourself aware of the numbers that are all around you – and use them as opportunities for practice:

- When you are shopping in the supermarket, estimate your total bill or continually calculate how much you can save by buying one product rather than another, or the cost of a single item contained in a multi-pack, or the cost per 100 mls or 100 grams based on a larger packet or container.

- Notice the data that is presented to you every day in the financial pages of newspapers. This will involve increases, decreases and percentages.

- Seek out numerical information in company reports or in trade magazines.

- Use train timetables to gain familiarity with using information presented in this way.

- Practise using currency exchange rates given in newspapers or by your travel agent.

- Brush up on using fractions, square roots, multiplication tables, percentages, and decimals.

If you usually use a calculator, put it away and practise without it. You will not be allowed to use one at the assessment centre.

THE TEST ITSELF

Tests will be timed and not much time will be allowed for you to do the tests, and it is frequently not possible to complete all the tests in the time allotted. Do not let this worry you.

Even when you are sitting in the test room, you can still improve your chances of success. There are a few important things to remember at this stage:

- Listen to – and be sure to comply with – the instructions given by the test administrator
- Read the instructions on the test paper – these may cover items such as:
  - How much time you will be allowed
  - Whether or not you may write on the margins of the test paper or if rough paper is supplied for your workings
  - How you should indicate your answer – with a tick or a cross, for example
  - What to do if you want to change one of your answers

If you don't understand something at this stage – before the test begins – speak up. There are sometimes example questions that you will be instructed to read before the timed test begins. Use the time allowed for this to ensure that you understand exactly what you are being asked to do. Don't try to pretend that you know everything – you do not need to impress the other candidates.

Read the questions carefully. Although you will be trying to work quickly, there is no point in answering all the questions but getting many of them wrong because you did not understand what was required.

Go through the questions methodically – don't be tempted to rush on to later questions first. Some papers may be structured so that the questions get progressively more difficult – if you look at the later questions first, you may not make the best use of your time.

STRATEGY

The main strategy during the test will involve timing (see below) but you may also want to consider how much you will use your powers of estimation. Here again, practice will help. Some questions on a numerical reasoning test are ideal for estimation. Rounding up or down can often be a quick way of arriving at the only possible answer from those given in multiple-choice questions.

If you are really struggling with a particular question, do not waste time. Finding a difficult question can be unnerving. Far better to move on – there may be later questions that you find easy.

Try not to let people around you affect your performance. Just because the person at the next desk to you has turned over a lot more pages than you, it does not mean that you are doing badly. They might have all their answers wrong!

TIMING

The time allowed for the various tests that you will undertake will range from 12 minutes for a numerical reasoning test to 25 minutes for a verbal logical reasoning test.

The important thing is to use your time wisely. It is rare that too much time will be allowed for a test. It is far more likely that you will run out of time. You will therefore need to work quickly while trying to be as accurate as possible. Try not to let one question take up too much of your time. If a particular question is proving difficult for you, move on. You can always come back to it if you find that you have plenty of time.

ON THE DAY

You must plan to arrive at the test centre in a state that is conducive to achieving your best possible score. This means being calm and focused. It is possible that you may feel nervous before the test, but you can help yourself by preparing in advance the practical details that will enable you to do well. Remember, it is unlikely that you are the only person who is feeling nervous; what is important is how you deal with your nerves! The following suggestions may help you to overcome unnecessary test-related anxiety.

1   Know where the test centre is located, and estimate how long it will take you to get there – plan your 'setting off time'. Now plan to leave 45 minutes before your setting off time to allow for travel delays. This way, you can be more or less certain that you will arrive at the test centre in good time. If, for any reason, you think you will miss the start of the session, call the administrator to ask for instructions.

2   Try to get a good night's sleep before the test. This is obvious advice and, realistically, it is not always possible, particularly if you are prone to nerves the night before a test. However, you can take some positive steps to help. Consider taking a hot bath before you go to bed, drinking herbal rather than caffeinated tea, and doing some exercise. Think back to what worked last time you took an exam and try to replicate the scenario.

3   The night before the test, organise everything that you need to take with you. This includes test instructions, directions, your identification, pens, erasers, plus your reading glasses and contact lenses if necessary.

4 Decide what you are going to wear and have your clothes ready the night before. Be prepared for the test centre to be unusually hot or cold, and dress in layers so that you can regulate the climate yourself. If your test will be preceded or followed by an interview, make sure you dress accordingly for the interview which is likely to be a more formal event than the test itself.

5 Eat breakfast! Even if you usually skip breakfast, you should consider that insufficient sugar levels affect your concentration and that a healthy breakfast might help you to concentrate, especially towards the end of the test when you are likely to be tired.

6 If you know that you have specific or exceptional requirements which will require preparation on the day, be sure to inform the test administrators in advance so that they can assist you as necessary. Similarly, if you are feeling unusually unwell on the day of the test, make sure that the test administrator is aware of it.

7 If, when you read the test instructions, there is something you don't understand, ask for clarification from the administrator. The time given to you to read the instructions may or may not be limited but, within the allowed time, you can usually ask questions. Don't assume that you have understood the instructions if, at first glance, they appear to be similar to the instructions for the practice tests.

8 Don't read through all the questions before you start. This simply wastes time. Start with Question 1 and work swiftly and methodically through each question in order. Unless you are taking a computerised test where the level of difficulty of the next question depends on you correctly answering the previous question, don't waste time on questions that you know require a lot of time. You can return to these questions at the end if you have time left over.

9 After you have taken the test, find out the mechanism for feedback, and approximately the number of days you will have to wait to find out your results. Ask whether there is scope for objective feedback on your performance for your future reference.

10 Celebrate that you have finished.

FURTHER SOURCES OF PRACTICE

In this final section, you will find a list of useful sources for all types of psychometric tests.

BOOKS

Bolles, Richard N., *What Color Is Your Parachute?* Berkeley, CA: Ten Speed Press, 2007.

Carter, P. and K. Russell, *Psychometric Testing: 1000 Ways to Assess Your Personality, Creativity, Intelligence and Lateral Thinking*. Chichester: John Wiley, 2001.

Jackson, Tom, *The Perfect Résumé*. New York: Broadway Books, 2004.

Kourdi, Jeremy, *Succeed at Psychometric Testing: Practice Tests for Verbal Reasoning Advanced*. London: Hodder Education, 2008.

Krannich, Ronald L. and Caryl Rae Krannich, *Network Your Way to Job and Career Success*. Manassa, VA: Impact Publications, 1989.

Nuga, Simbo, *Succeed at Psychometric Testing: Practice Tests for Verbal Reasoning Intermediate*. London: Hodder Education, 2008.

Rhodes, Peter, *Succeed at Psychometric Testing: Practice Tests for Critical Verbal Reasoning*. London: Hodder Education, 2008.

Rhodes, Peter, *Succeed at Psychometric Testing: Practice Tests for Diagrammatic and Abstract Reasoning*. London: Hodder Education, 2008.

Vanson, Sally, *Succeed at Psychometric Testing: Practice Tests for Data Interpretation*. London: Hodder Education, 2008.

Walmsley, Bernice, *Succeed at Psychometric Testing: Practice Tests for Numerical Reasoning Advanced*. London: Hodder Education, 2008.

Walmsley, Bernice, *Succeed at Psychometric Testing: Practice Tests for Numerical Reasoning Intermediate*. London: Hodder Education, 2008.

TEST PUBLISHERS AND SUPPLIERS

ASE
Chiswick Centre
414 Chiswick High Road
London W4 5TF
telephone: 0208 996 3337
www.ase-solutions.co.uk

Oxford Psychologists Press
Elsfield Hall
15–17 Elsfield Way
Oxford OX2 8EP
telephone: 01865 404500
www.opp.co.uk

Psytech International Ltd
The Grange
Church Road
Pulloxhill
Bedfordshire MK45 5HE
telephone: 01525 720003
www.psytech.co.uk

SHL
The Pavilion
1 Atwell Place
Thames Ditton
Surrey KT7 0SR
telephone: 0208 398 4170
www.shl.com

The Psychological Corporation
Harcourt Assessment
Halley Court
Jordan Hill
Oxford OX2 8EJ
www.tpc-international.com

The Test Agency Ltd
Burgner House
4630 Kingsgate
Oxford Business Park South
Oxford OX4 2SU
telephone: 01865 402900
www.testagency.com

OTHER USEFUL WEBSITES

Websites are prone to change, but the following are correct at the time of going to press.

www.careerpsychologycentre.com

www.cipd.org.uk

www.deloitte.co.uk/index.asp

www.ets.org

www.freesat1prep.com

www.mensa.org.uk

www.morrisby.co.uk

www.newmonday.co.uk

www.oneclickhr.com

www.pgcareers.com/apply/how/recruitment.asp

www.psychtesting.org.uk

www.psychtests.com

www.publicjobs.gov.ie

www.puzz.com

www.testagency.co.uk

www.tests-direct.com

OTHER USEFUL ORGANISATIONS

American Psychological Association Testing and Assessment – www.apa.org/science/testing

Association of Recognised English Language Schools (ARELS) – www.englishuk.com

Australian Psychological Society – www.psychology.org.au

The Best Practice Club – www.bpclub.com

The British Psychological Society – www.bps.org.uk

Canadian Psychological Association – www.cpa.ca

The Chartered Institute of Marketing – www.cim.co.uk

The Chartered Institute of Personnel and Development – www.cipd.co.uk

The Chartered Management Institute – www.managers.org.uk

Psyconsult – www.psyconsult.co.uk

Singapore Psychological Society – www.singaporepsychologicalsociety.co.uk

Society for Industrial and Organisational Assessment (South Africa) (SIOPSA) – www.siposa.org.za